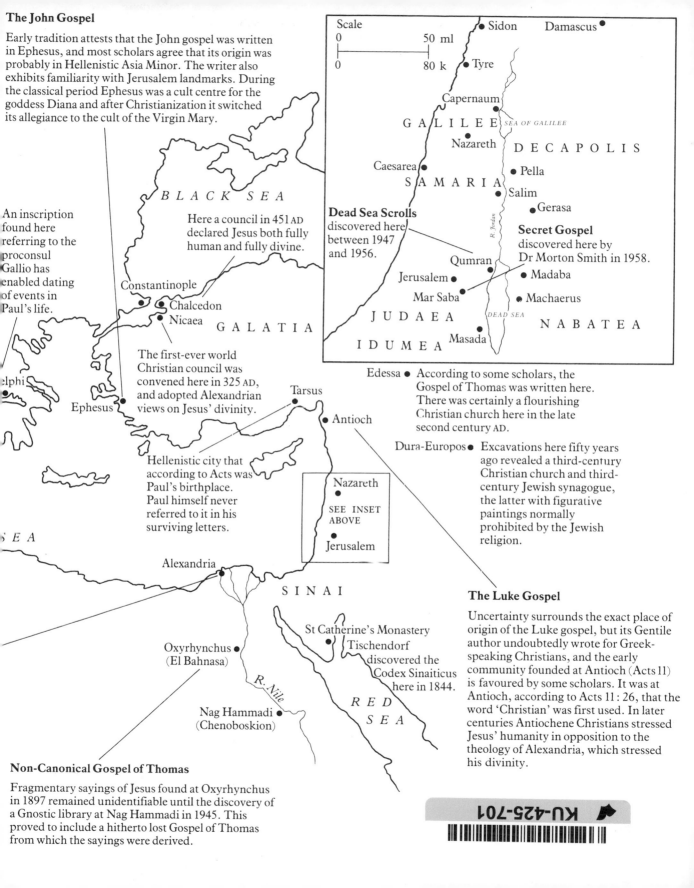

The John Gospel

Early tradition attests that the John gospel was written in Ephesus, and most scholars agree that its origin was probably in Hellenistic Asia Minor. The writer also exhibits familiarity with Jerusalem landmarks. During the classical period Ephesus was a cult centre for the goddess Diana and after Christianization it switched its allegiance to the cult of the Virgin Mary.

An inscription found here referring to the proconsul Gallio has enabled dating of events in Paul's life.

Here a council in 451 AD declared Jesus both fully human and fully divine.

The first-ever world Christian council was convened here in 325 AD, and adopted Alexandrian views on Jesus' divinity.

Hellenistic city that according to Acts was Paul's birthplace. Paul himself never referred to it in his surviving letters.

Scale
0 — 50 ml
0 — 80 k

Dead Sea Scrolls discovered here between 1947 and 1956.

Secret Gospel discovered here by Dr Morton Smith in 1958.

Edessa ● According to some scholars, the Gospel of Thomas was written here. There was certainly a flourishing Christian church here in the late second century AD.

Dura-Europos ● Excavations here fifty years ago revealed a third-century Christian church and third-century Jewish synagogue, the latter with figurative paintings normally prohibited by the Jewish religion.

The Luke Gospel

Uncertainty surrounds the exact place of origin of the Luke gospel, but its Gentile author undoubtedly wrote for Greek-speaking Christians, and the early community founded at Antioch (Acts 11) is favoured by some scholars. It was at Antioch, according to Acts 11 : 26, that the word 'Christian' was first used. In later centuries Antiochene Christians stressed Jesus' humanity in opposition to the theology of Alexandria, which stressed his divinity.

St Catherine's Monastery
Tischendorf discovered the Codex Sinaiticus here in 1844.

Non-Canonical Gospel of Thomas

Fragmentary sayings of Jesus found at Oxyrhynchus in 1897 remained unidentifiable until the discovery of a Gnostic library at Nag Hammadi in 1945. This proved to include a hitherto lost Gospel of Thomas from which the sayings were derived.

JESUS
THE EVIDENCE

JESUS
THE EVIDENCE

IAN WILSON

GUILD PUBLISHING
LONDON

This edition published 1984 by
Book Club Associates
by arrangement with Weidenfeld and Nicolson
in association with NB Productions

Printed and bound in Great Britain
by Butler & Tanner Ltd, Frome and London

CONTENTS

AUTHOR'S PREFACE

JESUS: THE EVIDENCE came into being through an unexpected and welcome invitation from London Weekend Television to write a book to accompany their three-part film series of the same name. While this was of course an irresistible challenge, involving the study and assessment of the facts surrounding a man who is perhaps the most controversial and influential figure in all history, the task has had its difficulties, not the least of them being matching the timing and content of the television production and attempting to be fair to both historical and Christian viewpoints. As has been remarked by Michael Green of my own university city, 'couple historical scepticism with a Christian profession, and it tears a man apart ...'

Too often Christian writers have neglected Jesus' essential Jewishness, and this is one deficiency I have especially tried to rectify. In this aim I have greatly valued the encouragement of Jewish scholars Dr Geza Vermes and Victor Tunkel, both of whom kindly read and advised on the manuscript. I am also deeply grateful to David Rolfe and Julian Norridge of London Weekend Television through whom the whole project came into being, to Ray Bruce and Arthur Rowe of I.L.E.A., who advised from the Christian point of view, to Dr T.S. Pattie of the British Museum Department of Manuscripts, who helped with the chart on pp 18–19, to my editor Wendy Dallas for her seemingly limitless care and patience in steering the book to publication, to Hazel Allinson, Debbie Hall, Jean-Claude Bragard, Peter Casson, Leonard Gould, Robert Smith, Dr Albert Mason, Dr Frederick Zugibe, Dr Alan Whanger, my father, and innumerable others for a variety of favours, and not least to picture researcher Caroline Lucas for her assiduous hunting down of some particularly obscure photographs. The task of picture selection was made harder by the self-imposed discipline of opting always for the nearest contemporary material, meaning automatic rejection of Old Masters, however beautiful. For most biblical quotations the Jerusalem Bible has been chosen because of its clear modern English, although

7

to avoid confusion 'God' has been substituted for 'Yahweh' in some Old Testament passages.

More than any other, the one man I wanted to advise on the manuscript of this book was the late Dr John Robinson, author of the controversial *Honest to God*, whom I had come to know through a shared interest in the Turin Shroud. Sadly, he was found to have inoperable cancer the very week the first draft was sent to him, and I insisted that he should not involve himself. I make no pretence even to begin to approach his erudition, but I have tried, however inadequately, to follow his spirit of sound common sense.

Bristol, England
January 1984

INTRODUCTION

> We believe in one Lord, Jesus Christ
> the only Son of God,
> eternally begotten of the Father
> God from God, Light from Light,
> true God from true God,
> begotten, not made,
> of one Being with the Father.
> Through him all things were made . . .

EVERY week, in Christian churches throughout the world, countless Protestant, Roman Catholic and Eastern Orthodox believers, in surprising unity, repeat this formula, the so-called Nicene Creed. It represents part of their common profession of faith. Although few reflect on it this way, it also represents the point of division between Christianity and every other form of belief. While Jews and Moslems would have little difficulty in accepting the immediately preceding words,

> We believe in one God,
> the Father, the Almighty,
> maker of heaven and earth . . .

(although Moslems would tend to balk at the concept of God as 'Father'), those relating to Jesus are of a different order. They demand the belief that a man who to all appearances was merely an obscure Jewish teacher of two thousand years ago, has in fact been co-creator and co-ruler of our multi-million galaxy universe throughout its entire existence. Such a concept has not only been dismissed as hopelessly irrational by atheists and agnostics, it has also quite understandably been rejected by Jews and Moslems as incompatible with their fundamental belief in the singularity of God.

To what extent should even a Christian cling to such a formula as a true expression of his or her beliefs? The Nicene Creed, which even the great

The Council of Nicaea, assembled by Constantine to decide matters of disagreement between fourth-century Christians. From a ninth-century manuscript.

Martin Luther (1483–1546), who questioned ecclesiastical authority and insisted on biblical texts becoming available in laymen's language. From a contemporary woodcut depicting him as the gospel-writer Matthew working on his translation of the scriptures.

Martin Luther left unscathed, is to be found in no gospel. It derives from no recorded utterances of Jesus, some of the remarks attributed to him being, in fact, in direct contradiction to its message. As is well known, the Creed sprang from a bitter theological feud, the Arian controversy, which raged during the fourth and fifth centuries AD. When it was first formulated at the Council of Nicaea in 325 AD, following the Roman Emperor Constantine the Great's apparent conversion to Christianity, not a few people felt that something of the original Jesus and the spirit of his teaching had been fatally compromised. The die had, however, been cast. It would become the norm for matters of individual Christian belief to be decided by a council of bishops, and the Nicene Creed reached its near final form in 451 AD at the Council of Chalcedon, when it was agreed by both Eastern and Western bishops that Jesus had been fully human and fully divine. In Rome it gradually became established that one man, the Bishop of Rome, had the right to make decisions for all Christendom. Those in the East objected to the idea of Roman supremacy and went their own ways, but in the West Christian doctrinal practice remained intact until the sixteenth century, when the great Martin Luther issued his challenge by nailing up his ninety-five theses on the door of the Schlosskirche at Wittenberg. Even when he did so his 'protest' was against the prevailing ecclesiastical authority rather than the basis of its theology. The Nicene formula was left unscathed.

Yet, as he could perhaps never have anticipated in his lifetime, Luther had set in train a whole new wave of critical attitudes towards some of the most fundamental tenets of Christian belief, even among those well placed within the Christian Church. Such criticism was particularly strong among Luther's own countrymen, some of whom, during the last century, even sacrificed academic preferment in their earnest endeavours to reach the real truth about Jesus.

In an age less fettered by dogma, we are the enlightened beneficiaries of those endeavours. Our knowledge of the life and times of Jesus has also been immensely enriched by recent discoveries from Israeli archaeology, from chance manuscript finds, from the researches of independent-minded Jewish scholars, and, not least, from a greater understanding of human psychology. So who exactly was Jesus? Did he even exist? What did he really teach? Would he have been prepared to endorse the Nicene decision? Or might he have found himself more at home in modern Judaism? It is in an honest, fair-minded attempt to answer these questions and more that *Jesus: the Evidence* has been written.

DISCOVERING THE
DOCUMENTS

THE quest for the earliest evidence for Jesus may be said to have begun, appropriately enough, with a party of men on camels, wending their way across the desert. It was a thoroughly biblical desert, the scorching wilderness of the Sinai, in whose granite cliffs Moses was said to have received the Ten Commandments, and Mahomet's camel to have left its footprint before transporting the prophet to heaven. The landscape had changed so little in the intervening centuries that such events might have happened yesterday.

The European seated on one of the camels was thirty-year-old Constantin Tischendorf, specialist in ancient languages from Germany, and the date was May 1844. Tischendorf's search, which had just brought him on a twelve-day trek across some of the most desolate terrain on earth, was for Christianity's most ancient documents. No destination could have seemed more formidable, yet promising, than the fortress-like building that he and his guides now approached, the Monastery of St Catherine, Sinai, hardly altered since first built by the Byzantine Emperor Justinian early in the sixth century AD. At first, as the caravan party halted, it seemed as if the monastery had been abandoned. No gates were thrown open to welcome the parched and dusty travellers. The walls, four storeys high, did not even seem to have any gates. But at last, after much shouting, a rope basket was lowered for Tischendorf's letters of introduction, and after a delay a second basket for the transport of Tischendorf himself. As an ancient hoist turned somewhere within, he found himself bumped precariously upwards, over the walls and into a world that time seemed to have abandoned long ago.

The monastery's black-robed monks received their visitor with typically Eastern Orthodox warmth and hospitality, and in the days that followed Tischendorf was allowed unrestricted access to the community's three libraries. He had developed a keen eye for the type of documents he was looking for. Back in the early sixteenth century, as part of the tide of interest in the original text of the New Testament generated by the Reformation, the great Dutch scholar Erasmus had compiled the first-ever printed edition of the New Testament in its original Greek. But by Tischendorf's time it had become increasingly recognized that the manuscripts Erasmus drew upon were those written in minuscule, that is upper and lower case Greek letters, a form of writing not developed until the ninth century AD. The characteristic feature of manuscripts written before the ninth century was handwriting in uncials, that is upper case or capital Greek letters only. Other stylistic traits made it possible to establish dating to the nearest century. But very early manuscripts were rare, and often presented considerable difficulties. Shortly before his travels to the Sinai, Tischendorf had spent two years working in Paris on the *Codex Ephraemi*, a so-called palimpsest, the original fifth-century scriptural text having been scraped away in the twelfth century in order that the expensive vellum could be re-used for the copying of some sermons. Although it had previously been thought impossible to retrieve *Ephraemi*'s original text, Tischendorf, resorting to simple devices such as holding the pages to the light, managed to accomplish the task within two years. Even older than *Ephraemi* was the Vatican's fourth-century *Codex Vaticanus*. But this presented difficulties of a different kind. Although Tischendorf travelled to Rome to study the manuscript, and was received kindly by Pope Gregory XVI, a jealous cardinal denied him access to it for any longer than six hours, time for nothing but the most hasty and tantalizing examination.

It was because of such problems that Tischendorf turned his sights to seeking out whatever manuscripts, possibly yet more ancient, might be lying unrecognized in the great eastern monasteries. That such establishments could contain material of this kind had long been known from travellers' tales. In 1677, at Mount Athos, British Ambassador Dr John Covel had come across 'vast heaps . . . all covered over with dust and dirt, many of them rotted and spoiled.' At the same monastery, a mere decade before Tischendorf's visit, British aristocrat Robert Curzon had come across a discarded page in uncial handwriting lying in an obviously neglected room. Asking if he might take it, the abbot enquired the reason for his request. 'My servant suggested that perhaps it might be useful to cover some jampots or vases of preserves which I have at home', lied Curzon. The abbot concurred and to Curzon's astonishment thereupon cut off an inch-thick wad of some other early manuscript pages for his distinguished visitor.

Against the background of such stories Tischendorf initially found his preliminary inspection of St Catherine's libraries somewhat disappointing. Then, as he subsequently recounted:

The Monastery of St Catherine on the slopes of Mount Sinai. It was here in 1844 that Constantin Tischendorf discovered the *Codex Sinaiticus*.

Constantin Tischendorf (1815-74), from a lithograph by Schneller.

The *Codex Sinaiticus*. From characteristics of the uncial
handwriting, scholars date its composition to the mid-fourth
century. With the *Codex Vaticanus*, it remains the earliest near
complete biblical text. Some missing pages were found only
recently at St Catherine's Monastery.

I perceived in the middle of the great hall a large and wide basket full of old parchments; and the librarian, who was a man of information, told me that two heaps of papers like these, mouldered by time, had already been committed to the flames. What was my surprise to find amid this heap of papers a considerable number of sheets of a copy of the Old Testament in Greek, which seemed to me to be one of the most ancient that I had ever seen. The authorities of the monastery allowed me to possess myself of a third of these parchments, or about forty-three sheets, all the more readily as they were destined for the fire. But I could not get them to yield up possession of the remainder. The too lively satisfaction which I displayed aroused their suspicions as to the value of this manuscript.

In betraying that the material was of considerable interest to him, Tischendorf had made the mistake which Robert Curzon, somewhat deviously, had avoided. On Tischendorf's next visit to St Catherine's the very existence of the parchments was denied. It was to take another fifteen years, and the leverage of credentials provided by Tsar Alexander II of Russia, before the monks were prepared to receive him again. It was with renewed warmth this time, because of his high-ranking introduction, and he was admitted by a secret door reserved only for the most distinguished visitors. Tischendorf was invited to enjoy a glass of the monastery's home-brewed date liqueur in the steward's cell, then with the words, 'And I too have read a Septuagint' (a Greek translation of the Old Testament), the steward suddenly walked across the room, lifted a cloth-wrapped bundle from a shelf, and laid this before his guest. To Tischendorf's astonishment, as he removed the covering he recognized,

... not only those very leaves which, fifteen years before, I had taken out of the basket, but also other parts of the Old Testament, the New Testament complete, and in addition the Epistle of Barnabas and a part of the Shepherd of Hermas. Full of joy, which this time I had the self-command to conceal from the steward and the rest of the community, I asked, as if in a careless way, for permission to take the manuscript into my sleeping chamber to look over it more at leisure. There by myself I could give way to the transport of joy which I felt. I knew that I held in my hand the most precious Biblical treasure in existence – a document whose age and importance exceeded that of all the manuscripts which I had ever examined during twenty years' study of the subject.

It is now well known that the manuscript which Tischendorf so emotionally leafed through that night, there and then transcribing the hitherto lost 'Epistle of Barnabas' and 'Shepherd' of Hermas, was what we know today as the *Codex Sinaiticus*.

Tischendorf borrowed the manuscript (he is often unfairly accused of having stolen it), and subsequently acted as intermediary for Tsar Alexander's purchase of it from St Catherine's monastery. In 1933, by which time it had fallen into Soviet ownership, it was bought by the British Museum from the then impecunious Communist government for the astronomic sum of £100,000, at that time by far the largest amount ever paid for a manuscript. Modern scholarship recognizes *Sinaiticus* as a sister manuscript to *Vaticanus* in that they share such textual peculiarities as an absence of the last eleven verses of the Mark gospel and omission of the John gospel story of the woman taken in adultery. Both manuscripts date from approximately the mid-fourth century, and remain the oldest near complete texts of Old and New Testaments in existence. Written on expensive vellum – *Sinaiticus* alone required the skins of 360 young sheep and goats – with little doubt they were the products of rich patronage of Christianity following Constantine the Great's conversion and the Council of Nicaea in 325 AD.

Today, thanks to modern archaeology (not to mention the enterprise of some sharp-eyed Moslem peasants), the antiquity of Christian documentation has been pushed back to at least two centuries before Nicaea, further back, indeed, than Tischendorf might ever have dared to hope. As might be expected of times when Christianity was the religion of the poor and the oppressed, a characteristic feature of this early documentation is its use of cheap papyrus paper, which has not helped its survival; Egypt, with its dry climate, is the only country in which significant quantities of such papyri have been found. Undoubtedly the material that has survived is genuinely early. Ancient documents often contain clues to when they were written, for example by references to an Emperor's reign, and by comparing their handwriting, punctuation, spacing and other characteristics with undated Christian manuscripts, it is often possible reliably to ascertain when the latter were written.

Unfortunately, because of the lure of more spectacular artefacts, interest in papyri was low during the days of early nineteenth-century Egyptology, and undoubtedly much ancient manuscript material, Christian or otherwise, would have been powdered to dust under untutored fellaheens' picks and spades. Only when, in 1883, the great Egyptologist Flinders Petrie, stumbling on some rubbish, fleetingly recognized amongst it before its disintegration a fragment of the 'finest Greek writing', was it realized that such material could have been preserved. In subsequent years Egyptian workmen, apprised of the worth of similar scraps of papyri, began turning up odd fragments, as a result of which in 1895, with great far-sightedness, the Egypt Exploration Fund decided to sponsor a young graduate who had worked

How a Christian scriptural manuscript can be dated

AD	HANDWRITING	OTHER CHARACTERISTIC FEATURES
1600 —	ERA OF PRINTING	1557 division into numbered verses by Robert Stephanus — ERA OF PAPER
1500 —		
1400 —		
1300 —	irregular, variegated lettering — PERIOD OF MINUSCULE* WRITING	
1200 —		c.1200 division into present-day chapters by Stephen Langton
1100 —		
1000 —	precise, upright lettering	PERIOD OF VELLUM (animal skin) CODICES
900 —	upright exaggerated lettering	breathing marks more regularly used
800 —	marked slope to right	introduction of comma
700 —		
600 —	letters ЄΘϹ upright ovals	
500 —	PERIOD OF UNCIAL† WRITING — vertical strokes thicken	5th c. introduction of dated colophons†† (initially in Syriac mss) — PERIOD OF PAPYRUS CODICES** (bound books)
400 —		early 4th c. New Testament books consistently titled & divided into sections; Eusebian cross-reference system introduced
300 —	Simple, dignified lettering	c.300 nut-gall & iron sulphate inks replace soot-based variety
200 —	letters ЄΘϹ circular	PERIOD OF PAPYRUS ROLLS**
100 —		

† Greek capital letters, e.g. ΤΑϹЄ

* Greek upper and lower case letters, e.g. Πυρίοισ

** Vellum was in use at this period, but is unknown for surviving Christian documents, no doubt because of expense (although 3rd-c. epistle of Hebrews written on back of vellum roll)

Surviving Christian manuscripts and when they were written

CANONICAL			NON-CANONICAL	AD
LATIN	GREEK	OTHER	**17th c.** Mar Saba 'Secret gospel' of Mark transcription	— 1600
	1516 Erasmus' first printed edition			— 1500
1455 Gutenburg's first printed Vulgate				— 1400
	c. 4000 SURVIVING MINUSCULE MSS (but few of complete Bible)			— 1300
				— 1200
ERA OF THE LATIN VULGATE				— 1100
				— 1000
	835 first surviving dated minuscule of gospels	**897** earliest Georgian mss of gospels	COPYING OF NUMEROUS APOCRYPHAL MSS (begun at very early date)	— 900
		887 earliest Armenian mss of gospels		— 800
716 earliest extant Vulgate of complete Bible	*c.* 270 SURVIVING UNCIAL MSS (but few complete)	**5th/6th c.** earliest Gothic mss of gospels		— 700
541-6 Codex Fuldensis	**early 5th c.** Codex Ephraemi	**5th c.** Coptic gospels of Mark & Luke (Barcelona)		— 600
late 5th c. Codex Sangallensis of gospels				— 500
	4th c. Codex Vaticanus; Codex Sinaiticus	**4th c.** Coptic Deuteronomy, Jonah & Acts	**4th c.** Achmim 'Gospel of Peter'; Nag Hammadi Gnostic hoard & 'Thomas' gospel	— 400
	3rd c. Chester Beatty papyri of most New Testament books; Bodmer papyrus fragments from Luke and John gospels		**3rd c.** Dura fragment of Tatian harmony of canonical gospels	— 300
				— 200
	early 2nd c. Rylands fragment of John gospel		**mid-2nd c.** Egerton papyrus of unknown gospel; Oxyrhynchus fragment of 'Thomas' gospel	— 100

†† a colophon is a paragraph, usually found at the end of a manuscript, giving information about authorship, sources, etc.

Ⓝ the period of papyrus rolls lasted until the sixth century for literary works, as distinct from scriptural material with Petrie, Bernard Pyne Grenfell, to conduct a concentrated search for such material. Grenfell in his turn co-opted on to the assignment a college friend, Arthur Surridge Hunt. Although the partnership's first season in the Fayum was unrewarding, the next year they took the inspired decision to investigate the apparently totally unprepossessing Futuh el Bahnasa, site of the former Hellenistic settlement of Oxyrhynchus, where in antiquity there had been a long-abandoned complex of early Christian monasteries and churches. Since no papyrus finds had ever been heard of from Oxyrhynchus, Grenfell suspected that it might not have suffered from the plundering that occurred elsewhere. Even more inspired was his choice of where to dig. Ignoring the remains of the early church buildings, from which he antici-pated that anything of interest would have long since disappeared, he turned his attention to the seventy-foot-high ancient rubbish heaps that lay on the site's outskirts. To investigate these properly would require helpers, who would in turn require eagle-eyed supervision; undaunted, Grenfell pro-ceeded to hire a seventy-strong workforce to cut into the most promising looking mound. In his account of the dig he did not minimize its unpleasant-ness:

... standing all day to be half choked and blinded by the peculiarly pungent dust of ancient rubbish, blended on most days with the not less irritating sand of the desert; probably drinking water which not even the East London waterworks would have ventured to supply to its consumers, and keeping incessant watch over men who, however much you may flatter yourself to the contrary, will steal if they get the chance and think it worth their while to do so.

Despite such difficulties, the dig rapidly began to produce results, yielding papyrus scraps of considerable variety and quantity. Many of these were private letters, contracts and other legal or official documents, all of consider-able interest in illuminating the everyday life of antiquity. But also among them were fragments in the characteristic handwriting styles of early reli-gious and literary texts.

It was Hunt who, as soon as a substantial quantity of such material had accumulated, sat down to the task of preliminary sorting. Only two days later, carefully smoothing out a crumpled, six-inch by four-inch scrap that seemed to have come from a numbered, paged book (quite different, there-fore, from the long scrolls on which early Jewish and pagan religious litera-ture was written), his eye fell on the word *karphos*. He recognized this as the Greek word which is translated as 'mote' in the familiar King James Bible text:

Above Papyrologists Bernard Grenfell and Arthur Hunt, photographed during one of their digs at Oxyrhynchus. They discovered fragments of a hitherto unknown gospel of Jesus' sayings, dated *c.*200 AD, now known to derive from an early Greek version of a 'Gospel of Thomas'.

Right Fragment of the Thomas gospel from Oxyrhynchus. At the time of discovery this and accompanying fragments represented the earliest known documentary evidence for Jesus' existence, all the more remarkable for their inclusion of some hitherto unknown sayings. The unusual Greek word *karphos*, which first caught Hunt's attention, appears at the end of the main text's second line.

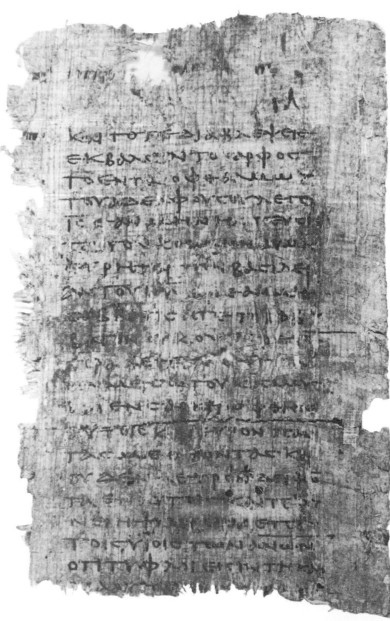

And why beholdest thou the mote that is in thy brother's eye, but considerest not the beam that is in thine own eye? (Matthew 7: 3–5; also Luke 6: 41).

As Hunt deciphered further, he recognized the fragment in his hand as being a version of the same well-known saying:

... then you will clearly see to cast the mote from your brother's eye

The form of words was significantly different from the known gospels, and as Hunt read on he realized that the scrap simply could not be from one of them. The fragment included seven sayings altogether, each preceded by the words 'Says Jesus'. Three of them had no obvious counterpart in any of the known gospels, yet they sounded as if they could have come from the mouth of the gospel Jesus. What is more, the style of uncials in which the sayings were written dated them to the work of a copyist of about 200 AD. Overnight the antiquity of *Sinaiticus* had been superseded by a non-canonical gospel text, and evidence of Jesus' existence supported by a piece of documentation from little more than a century and a half after the time he is said to have lived. A few further scraps from this same unknown gospel came to light in the course of Grenfell and Hunt's further excavations.

If such a discovery might have seemed to threaten the canonical gospels' priority, the balance was redressed during the 1930s when American mining millionaire Alfred Chester Beatty announced his acquisition, via the Egyptian black market, of fragmentary papyrus texts of most of the recognized books of the New Testament, including parts of the Matthew and John gospels, a little more of the Mark and Luke gospels, half of Acts, a third of Revelations, and some 86 pages from what had once been a 104-page booklet of Paul's epistles. Evidently they had originally been bound as a codex or booklet, like the pages found by Grenfell and Hunt, and the writing could be judged to be roughly contemporary. Most of these acquisitions are now preserved in the Chester Beatty Collection in Dublin, but some are in Michigan and Princeton University libraries and in the Austrian National Library, Vienna. During the 1950s a Swiss collector, Martin Bodmer, via the same sort of undercover deals as Chester Beatty's, acquired and made public substantial portions of a papyrus codex of the John and Luke gospels, again datable to around 200 AD.

Quite overshadowing such material, however, which attracted relatively little press attention, was the discovery in 1945, near the modern town of Nag Hammadi in Upper Egypt, of a manuscript hoard not only of substantial interest in itself but also including the vital key for identifying the mysterious gospel found by Grenfell and Hunt. A party of Arab peasants were digging for natural fertilizer around a huge boulder in the cave-dotted mountainside of Egypt's Jabal al-Tarif, some four hundred miles south of Oxyrhynchus, and they came across a large red earthenware jar, deeply sunk into the soil. Eagerly hoping for gold, one of the Arabs smashed the jar open with his mattock. To the group's disappointment, all that tumbled out was a collection of thirteen leather-bound papyrus books, together with some loose papyri. The loose sheets soon saw use as kindling, but a suspicion that the books might at least have some cash value led the peasants to approach the antiquities black market. After a few dubious adventures, the books eventually reached scholarly scrutiny. Written in Greek characters in Coptic (the latest form of the original Egyptian language), they turned out to be part of the library of one of the numerous Gnostic groups, who professed some secret knowledge of Jesus and were known to have proliferated in the first centuries of Christianity. In common with other known examples of such literature, many of the texts – an 'Apocalypse of Paul', a 'Letter of Peter to Philip', an 'Apocalypse of Peter', a 'Secret Book of James' – although professing apostolic authority, were all too obviously apocryphal. The collection could be judged to have been written during the early fourth century, and was almost certainly buried during the latter half, when Christianity, having gained official status, began to purge its own fringe groups.

But in one booklet was a text with a distinctly different and arguably more credible ring than most of the rest. Even the opening words were intriguing: 'These are the secret sayings which the living Jesus spoke, and which Didymos Judas Thomas wrote down.' A collection of some 114 sayings attributed to Jesus, it became swiftly recognized that this 'gospel of Thomas' could be none other than a complete Coptic version of the same gospel from which Grenfell and Hunt's Greek uncial fragments were derived, a gospel which, because of the Oxyrhynchus find, must date from at least as early as the late second century. The content was extremely simple, imparting no special titles to Jesus, containing no account of his crucifixion and resurrection, but embodying a fascinating collection of sayings attributed to him. Some were merely slight variants on those already known from the canonical gospels, others strange yet nonetheless credible. Much of the speech the Thomas gospel attributed to Jesus concerned the mysterious Kingdom of God or 'kingdom of heaven' so cryptically referred to in the gospels. Though a little more explicit, it was still enigmatic:

Jesus said, 'If those who lead you say to you, "See, the kingdom is in the sky", then the birds of the sky will precede you. If they say to you, "It is in the sea", then

Above The eighteenth-century transcription of a third-century letter apparently written by Clement of Alexandria. In it Clement speaks of a secret version of Mark's gospel (beginning four lines from foot of left-hand page as indicated by arrow) made available only to special initiates. Some reputable scholars accept the letter's authenticity, but the possibility remains that it is an elaborate hoax.

Left Dr Morton Smith of Columbia University who discovered the 'secret' version of the gospel of Mark at the desert monastery of Mar Saba.

Far left Mar Saba, twelve miles from Jerusalem.

the fish will precede you. Rather, the kingdom is inside of you and it is outside of you. When you come to know yourselves, then you will become known.'

Thomas introduces a number of themes that are unrepresented or merely hinted at in the canonical gospels, for example he suggests that Jesus had a strikingly modern attitude to nudity:

His disciples said 'When will you be revealed to us and when shall we see you?' Jesus said, 'When you disrobe without being ashamed and take up your garments and place them under your feet like little children, and tread on them ...'

To this day scholars puzzle over the exact significance of the gospel of Thomas and some of the other Gnostic material from Nag Hammadi. Contributing further to the confusion is a surprising discovery made by Dr Morton Smith, today Professor of Ancient History at Columbia University, New York. In 1941, while still a university student, Smith found himself stranded in Palestine as a result of the Second World War. Befriended by a kindly Greek Orthodox monk, he was invited to stay for a few weeks at the monastery of Mar Saba, twelve miles from Jerusalem and, with St Catherine's, one of the two great desert monasteries of the Eastern Orthodox Church. Deeply impressed by the almost hypnotic quality of the Orthodox liturgy, Smith was delighted when in 1958 he was invited to return to Mar Saba to study and catalogue its collection of manuscripts. It was in the course of this task, carefully checking even printed books for stray manuscript inserts and the like, that Smith found himself incredulously deciphering tiny handwriting scrawled on the endpaper of a seventeenth-century edition of the letters of St Ignatius of Antioch. It was the text of a letter, and although from the handwriting it must have been written around the mid-eighteenth century, it appeared to have been copied from a letter of the early Church father Clement of Alexandria, who lived at the end of the second century AD. Addressed to a certain 'Theodore', Clement's letter spoke of a 'secret' gospel of Mark, based on the normal canonical one but with additions designed for certain special followers of Jesus, variously referred to as 'those who were being perfected' and 'those who are being initiated into the great mysteries'. The letter went so far as to quote extracts from the secret version of Mark, revealing it to have contained what appeared to be an account of the 'raising of Lazarus'. Although not directly named as Lazarus, but referred to as the rich young man mentioned elsewhere in the gospels, he is described as 'dying', being buried and then brought back to life by Jesus:

And they came into Bethany, and a certain woman, whose brother had died, was there. And, coming, she prostrated herself before Jesus and says to him, 'Son of

David, have mercy on me'. But the disciples rebuked her. And Jesus, being angered, went off with her into the garden where the tomb was, and straightway a great cry was heard from the tomb. And going near, Jesus rolled away the stone from the door of the tomb. And straightway, going in where the youth was, he stretched forth his hand and raised him, seizing his hand. But the youth, looking upon him, loved him and began to beseech him that he might be with him. And going out of the tomb they came into the house of the youth, for he was rich. And after six days Jesus told him what to do and in the evening the youth comes to him, wearing a linen cloth over [his] naked [body]. And he remained with him that night, for Jesus taught him the mystery of the kingdom of God. And thence, arising, he returned to the other side of the Jordan.

Clement follows up the quotation with a reassurance that there is nothing in the 'secret gospel' to justify the rumours that 'Theodore' (the recipient of the letter) had obviously heard, that Jesus and the rich young man were naked together during the initiation. He also fills in what is an otherwise unexplained gap in verse 46 of the tenth chapter of the canonical Mark gospel: 'They reached Jericho; and as he left Jericho ...' For centuries scholars have puzzled over what might have happened in Jericho. According to the Clement letter, the secret gospel originally read: 'And the sister of the youth whom Jesus loved and his mother and Salome were there, and Jesus did not receive them.'

As Morton Smith recognized, the letter was astonishing because it not only represented Mark's gospel as having originally contained the Lazarus story (it is otherwise known only from the John gospel), it also seems to have appeared in Mark in a far more simple and primitive form than in John. The canonical Mark is in general regarded by scholars as having been written earlier than John. Arguably, therefore, this secret version was also older and possibly more accurate. Its discovery also provided a perfect explanation for another baffling episode in the canonical Mark gospel, the fact that at the time of Jesus' arrest in Gethsemane:

A young man who followed him had nothing on but a linen cloth. They caught hold of him, but he left the cloth in their hands and ran away naked. (Mark 14: 51, 52)

If this letter *is* a copy of one written by Clement, and most modern scholars concur that it is, then this new information, independent of the canonical gospels, raises some intriguing questions concerning the founder of Christianity.

[... they urged] the crowd to [pick up] stones and stone him. And the leading men would have arrested him to [hand him over] to the crowd, but no-one could take him because the time of his betrayal had not yet come. So he, the Lord, that is, slipped away through their midst. A leper now came up and said 'Master Jesus, through travelling with lepers and eating with them at the inn I myself likewise became a leper. If you want to, you can cure me.' The Lord then said to him 'Of course I want to: be cured!' And his leprosy was cured at once. (Then Jesus said to him), 'Go (and show yourself) to the (priests ...'

Translation of a portion of the Egerton Papyrus 2, dating from not later than the mid-second century AD, and thereby the oldest non-canonical gospel document yet discovered. Elements of the Egerton text are also to be found in the canonical gospels, as for example the attempt to stone Jesus (John 7 & 8), and the healing of the leper (Matthew 8: 2–3; Mark 1: 40–2; Luke 5: 12–13). Although the differences in wording and sequence show that this cannot be from any canonical gospel, what has survived contains nothing of an obviously heretical nature.

Above The Gnostic gospels discovered at Nag Hammadi in 1945. Written in Coptic during the fourth century, many of these proved to be fanciful works of late composition. But among them was a complete text of the Thomas gospel fragments found by Grenfell and Hunt.

These are by no means the only hitherto unknown gospels that have come to light. The British Museum has two imperfect leaves and a scrap of papyrus, known by scholars as Egerton Papyrus 2, that appear to derive from a narrative work unlike the canonical gospels but with material closely based on theirs. Recognizable from these fragments are a near identical version of the Matthew, Mark and Luke accounts of the healing of a leper (Matthew 8: 2-3; Mark 1: 40-2; Luke 5: 12-13), together with a description of Jesus escaping stoning, similar to that in John 8: 59. Originally part of a papyrus book, the Egerton fragments, like the Chester Beatty and Oxyrhynchus material, were found in Egypt; the handwriting identifies them as certainly not later than 150 AD, and is closest in appearance to that of a non-Christian document datable precisely to 94 AD. Again we have the briefest glimpse of a gospel otherwise unknown to us.

The canonical gospel writer Luke mentions (1: 1, 2) that in his time there were 'many' other gospels in existence, most of which have unfortunately been lost to us. The writings of the early Church fathers provide clues to the existence of a few of these: a 'gospel of the Hebrews', evidently of a strongly Jewish character, mentioned by Origen and Jerome; a 'gospel according to the Egyptians', apparently somewhat ascetic, and favoured by Gentile Christians in Egypt, mentioned by Origen and Clement of Alexandria; and a 'gospel of the Ebionites', apparently strongly opposed to the writings of the apostle Paul, mentioned in a condemnation of heresies by the fourth-century writer Epiphanius. Clearly the manuscripts discovered so far are but a drop in the ocean of early documentary material circulated about Jesus.

Perhaps the most important of all discoveries to date has been that of an insignificant-looking two-and-a-half-inch by three-and-a-half-inch papyrus fragment of verses 37 and 38 from the eighteenth chapter of the John gospel, preserved today in the John Rylands Library of Manchester University. It was originally bought in Egypt in the early 1920s by Bernard Grenfell, but ill health prevented him from studying it thoroughly, and its full significance was not recognized until 1934, when it was examined by young Oxford University graduate Colin Roberts. From careful study of the handwriting, Roberts was able to date it to between 100 and 125 AD, well within a century of the time of Jesus, making it the earliest known identifiable fragment of the original New Testament. As Princeton University manuscript specialist Bruce Metzger has remarked:

Although the extent of the verses preserved is so slight, in one respect this tiny scrap of papyrus possesses as much evidential value as would the complete codex. As Robinson Crusoe, seeing but a single footprint in the sand, concluded that

The Rylands fragment, front and rear views. Analysis of the handwriting indicates that it was written within a century of Jesus' death. On the front (above) is the Greek text of John 18: 31-4; on the back (right) is John 18: 37-8. Because parts of the margins have been preserved, the original page can be calculated to have measured 21.5 × 20 cm, and would have formed part of a 130-page codex, or primitive book. (John Rylands Library, Manchester.)

another human being, with two feet, was present on the island with him, so 𝕡⁵² [the Rylands fragment's international code name], proves the existence and use of the Fourth Gospel in a little provincial town along the Nile far from its traditional place of composition (Ephesus in Asia Minor), during the first half of the Second Century.

What, then, have the documentary discoveries revealed? Just as the finding of the Dead Sea Scrolls demonstrated that the books of the Old Testament had suffered little textual change over many centuries, so the New Testament manuscript discoveries exhibit a reassuring general consistency. Hand-copying from one manuscript to another inevitably produces errors and misreadings, and it has been possible to trace the origins of whole families of texts – the Caesarean, the Byzantine, the Western and the Alexandrian – from the perpetuation of such peculiarities and errors in one community or region. The same tell-tale features also help to establish the date and authority of a particular text: for example, the authenticity of *Vaticanus* and *Sinaiticus* is supported by the fact that the Bodmer papyri has been found to be of the same Alexandrian text family. But on the whole, errors and textual variations are relatively minor, and the canonical gospels can be judged to be very much as their authors wrote them.

The sheer wealth of the early documentary material is one of its most impressive aspects. While of the works of the great Roman historian Tacitus there exists merely a copy of a single manuscript dating from about the twelfth century, of canonical works attesting to Jesus' existence there are some 274 vellum manuscripts, brothers and sisters of *Sinaiticus*, dating from between the fourth and eleventh centuries, and no less than 88 papyrus fragments datable to between the second and the fourth centuries. And this is quite independent of the intriguing non-canonical material to which further consideration will be given later in this book.

We can be sure that the gospel texts were genuinely early, and that their copyists were reasonably reliable, but what of the actual origination of the gospels? Who wrote them? And when? And even more crucially, how much can we trust them?

THE FALLIBILITY OF THE
GOSPELS

IT is perhaps a reflection of today's emphasis on a Jesus of faith that most modern Christians, practising and non-practising, are quite unaware of the sort of conflicts that have riven the world of gospel studies during the last century or so.

Few realize, for instance, that despite the fact that the canonical gospels bear the names Matthew, Mark, Luke and John, these names are mere attributions, and not necessarily those of their real authors. The earliest writers who referred to the gospels significantly failed to mention names of authors, it being apparent that each gospel, both those surviving and those that have failed to survive, was originally designed as *the* gospel for a particular community. A canon of the four 'recognized' gospels only gradually came into general usage, at the same time acquiring associations with specific names from Christianity's earliest years, though the connection was not necessarily legitimate. It should also be borne in mind that the earliest texts had none of the easy identification features that they bear now. Everything, without exception, was written in capital letters. There were no headings, chapter divisions or verse divisions, refinements which were not to appear until the Middle Ages. To make matters difficult even for the modern scholar, there was practically no punctuation or space between words.

Given such considerations it does not need anyone with a Ph.D. in theology to recognize that the Christian gospels can scarcely be the infallible works fundamentalists would have us believe. Examples of one gospel's inconsistency with another are easy enough to find. While according to the Mark and Luke gospels Jesus stayed in Peter's house, and afterwards healed the leper (Mark 1: 29–45; Luke 4: 38 ff; Luke 5: 12 ff), according to Matthew (8: 1–4 and 14 ff) Jesus healed the leper first. While according to Matthew the Capernaum centurion spoke man-to-man with Jesus (Matthew 8: 5 ff), according to Luke (7: 1 ff) he sent 'some Jewish elders' and friends to speak on his behalf. Although according to Acts Judas Iscariot died from an

David Friedrich Strauss (1808–74), lecturer at Tübingen University. He was dismissed from this post when, under the influence of contemporary rationalism, he rejected as spurious all supernatural elements in the gospel stories.

HERMANNUS SAMUEL REIMARUS
P. P. HAMB. AETATIS LVI.

Hermann Samuel Reimarus (1694–1768), Professor of Oriental Languages at Hamburg University, who wrote a secret work disputing the reliability of the gospel narratives. He gave instructions that this should only be published after his death.

Wilhelm Wrede (1859–1906), Professor of New Testament studies at Breslau University, Wrede argued that even in the Mark gospel, thought to be the most primitive, the author was more concerned with theological dogma than with historical accuracy.

Right Rudolf Bultmann (1884–1976), Professor of New Testament studies at Marburg University, who pioneered the 'form-criticism' method of analysing the gospels. He reached the view that very little of the gospel material could be relied upon.

accidental fall after betraying Jesus (Acts 1: 18), according to Matthew he 'went and hanged himself' (Matthew 27: 5).

Disconcerting though such inconsistencies are, the fair-minded sceptic might be disposed to regard them as no worse than the sort of reporting errors which occur daily in modern newspapers. But New Testament criticism has gone much deeper than pointing out flaws of this order, there having been, in some quarters at least, a fashion for each new critic to be bent on outdoing his predecessors in casting doubt on the gospels' authenticity.

The first forays into understanding the men and facts behind the gospels

The parallel passage technique

MARK 16: 2–5	LUKE 24: 1–4	MATTHEW 28: 1–4
. . . very early in the morning on the first day of the week they went to the tomb just as the sun was rising. They had been saying to one another 'Who will roll away the stone for us from the entrance to the tomb?' But when they looked they could see that the stone – which was very big – had already been rolled back. On entering the tomb they saw a young man in a white robe seated at the right-hand side.	On the first day of the week, at the first sign of dawn, they went to the tomb with the spices they had prepared. They found that the stone had been rolled away from the tomb, but on entering discovered that the body of the Lord Jesus was not there. As they stood there not knowing what to think, two men in brilliant clothes suddenly appeared at their side . . .	. . . towards dawn on the first day of the week Mary of Magdala and the other Mary went to visit the sepulchre. And all at once there was a violent earthquake, for the angel of the Lord, descending from heaven, came and rolled away the stone and sat on it. His face was like lightning, his robe white as snow . . .

Careful comparison of the three gospel passages above reveals a fundamental common ground – the time of morning, the day of the week, the rolling away of the stone, the visit to the tomb by women. But it also discloses some equally fundamental differences which serve to tell us something about the gospel writers. The Mark author, for instance, speaks merely of 'a young man in a white robe', with no suggestion that this individual was anything other than an ordinary human being. In the Luke version we find 'two men in brilliant clothes' who appear 'suddenly'. Although not absolutely explicit, there is already a strong hint of the supernatural. But for the Matthew writer, all restraints are abandoned. A violent earthquake has been introduced into the story, Mark's mere 'young man' has become a dazzling 'angel of the Lord . . . from heaven', and this explicitly extra-terrestrial visitor is accredited with the rolling away of the stone.

began harmlessly enough. Many incidents concerning Jesus are related in two or more of the gospels, and an early research technique, still extremely valuable, was to study the corresponding passages side by side, the so-called 'parallel passage' technique. This method is useful for showing up which episodes are common to all gospels, which are peculiar to a single gospel, the variations of interest or emphasis between one writer and another, and so on. It is immediately obvious that while Matthew, Mark and Luke have a great deal in common, describing the same 'miracles', the same sayings, essentially sharing a common narrative framework, the John gospel is a maverick, describing different incidents and devoting much space to lengthy, apparently verbatim speeches that seem quite unlike Jesus' pithy utterances reported elsewhere. In about 1774 the pioneering German scholar Johann Griesbach coined the word 'synoptic' for the Matthew, Mark and Luke gospels, from the Greek for 'seen together', while that of John has become generally known as the Fourth Gospel. It has always been regarded as having been written later than the other three.

As different theologians pursued the underlying clues to the gospel writers' psychology revealed by the parallel passage technique, so increasing scepticism developed, particularly in Germany during the early nineteenth century. There, a century earlier, a faltering start on a critical approach had been made by Hamburg University oriental languages professor Hermann Samuel Reimarus. In secret Reimarus wrote a book, *On the Aims of Jesus and his Disciples*, arguing that Jesus was merely a failed Jewish revolutionary, and that after his death his disciples cunningly stole his body from the tomb in order to concoct the whole story of his resurrection. So concerned was Reimarus to avoid recriminations for holding such views that he would only allow the book to be published after his death. His caution was justified. Following in the critical tradition, in the years 1835–6 Tübingen University tutor David Friedrich Strauss launched his two-volume *The Life of Jesus Critically Examined*, making particularly penetrating use of the parallel passage technique. Because of the discrepancies he found, he cogently argued that none of the gospels could have been by eyewitnesses, but instead must have been the work of writers of a much later generation, freely constructing their material from probably garbled traditions about Jesus in circulation in the early Church. Inspired by the materialistic rationalism of the philosophers Kant and Hegel – 'the real is the rational and the rational is the real' – Strauss uncompromisingly dismissed the gospel miracle stories as mere myths invented to give Jesus greater importance. For such findings Strauss was himself summarily dismissed from his tutorship at Tübingen, and later failed, for the same reason, to gain an important professorship at Zürich.

But the incursion into theology of the increasingly scientific outlook of the age was not to be checked so easily, particularly among Protestants. Under the professorship of the redoubtable Ferdinand Christian Baur, a prodigiously productive theologian who was at his desk by four o'clock each morning, Tübingen University in particular acquired a reputation for a ruthlessly iconoclastic approach to the New Testament, an approach which spread not only throughout Germany, but also into the universities of other predominantly Protestant countries. Traditionally the Matthew gospel had been regarded as the earliest of the four New Testament gospels, and it went virtually unquestioned that its author was Matthew, the tax-collector disciple of Jesus. In 1835 Berlin philologist Karl Lachmann argued forcefully that the Mark gospel, simpler and more primitive, was the earliest of the three synoptics. Lachmann became swiftly followed by scholars Weisse and Wilke, later in the century the argument was taken up by Heidelberg theologian Heinrich Holtzmann, and by the end of the century Mark's priority (even though not without challengers to this day) had become the most universally accepted theological discovery of the age.

And this raised immediate problems concerning the authorship of Matthew. The Mark gospel, which from internal and external clues was almost certainly written in Rome, ostensibly offers the least claim of all the synoptics to eyewitness reporting. Traditionally, Mark is claimed to have been at best some sort of secretary or interpreter for Peter. The connection with Peter, if it existed at all, cannot have been that close, however, for the Mark gospel exhibits a lamentable ignorance of Palestinian geography. In the seventh chapter, for instance, Jesus is reported as going through Sidon on his way to Tyre to the Sea of Galilee. Not only is Sidon in the opposite direction, but there was in fact no road from Sidon to the Sea of Galilee in the first century AD, only one from Tyre. Similarly the fifth chapter refers to the Sea of Galilee's eastern shore as the country of the Gerasenes, yet Gerasa, today Jerash, is more than thirty miles to the south-east, too far away for a story whose setting requires a nearby city with a steep slope down to the sea. Aside from geography, Mark represents Jesus as saying, 'If a woman divorces her husband and marries another she is guilty of adultery' (Mark 10:12), a precept which would have beeen meaningless in the Jewish world, where women had no rights of divorce. The author of the Mark gospel must have attributed the remark to Jesus for the benefit of Gentile readers.

Since it is demonstrable that the author of Matthew drew a substantial amount of his material from the Mark gospel, is is virtually impossible to believe that the original tax-collector Matthew, represented as having known Jesus at first hand, and having travelled with him, would have based his gospel on an inaccurate work whose author clearly had no such advantages. Bluntly, the original disciple Matthew could not have written the gospel that bears his name. Whoever wrote it must have been later than Mark. As a result of such reasoning, the German theologians began increasingly to date the origination of all three synoptic gospels to well into the second century AD.

In turn the John gospel came under similar scrutiny. The long speeches in fluent Greek attributed to Jesus were considered by German theologians to be Hellenistic in character, compatible with the gospel's traditional provenance, the Hellenistic city of Ephesus in Asia Minor. Since even Church tradition acknowledged the John gospel to have been written later than the rest, it was thought to be most likely to date from close to the end of the second century. However, the one apparent crumb of comfort, that the Mark gospel, despite its geographical flaws, seemed to offer a less fanciful version of Jesus' life than the rest, was in turn swept away with the publication, in 1901, of Breslau professor Wilhelm Wrede's *The Secret of the Messiahship*. Wrede argued powerfully that whoever wrote Mark tried to present Jesus as having deliberately made a secret of his Messiahship during his lifetime, and that most of his disciples failed to recognize him as the Messiah until after his death. While not necessarily giving this idea their full endorsement, most modern scholars acknowledge Wrede's insight in establishing one fundamental truth – that even the purportedly 'primitive' Mark gospel was more concerned with theology, with putting over a predetermined theological viewpoint, than with providing a straight historical narrative. Five years after Wrede's publication, in a closely written treatise *From Reimarus to Wrede*, translated into English as *The Quest for the Historical Jesus*, Albert Schweitzer, later to become the world-famous Lambarene missionary, summarized the work of his fellow German theological predecessors in these terms:

There is nothing more negative than the result of the critical study of the life of Jesus. The Jesus of Nazareth who came forward publicly as the Messiah, who preached the ethic of the Kingdom of God, who founded the Kingdom of Heaven upon earth, and died to give his work its final consecration, never had any existence ... This image has not been destroyed from without, it has fallen to pieces, cleft and disintegrated by the concrete historical problems which came to the surface one after another ...

If all these new discoveries seemed damaging enough, within two decades on to the scene at Germany's Marburg University stepped Rudolf Bultmann, acknowledged by many as this century's greatest New Testament theologian, bringing with him a new and yet more devastating weapon, *Formgeschichte* or 'form criticism'. This followed on from the work of Karl Ludwig Schmidt, a German pastor who had noted that a particular weakness of gospels such as Mark's lay in the link passages, which appeared to have been invented to give an impression of continuity between one episode or saying and the next. Bultmann set his sights to trying to reconstruct what material, if any, might be authentic between the links. His approach was to try to assess each gospel element – birth story, miracle story, ethical saying, etc. – in order to establish whether it was original or had been borrowed from the Old Testament, or from contemporary Jewish thought, or merely invented to suit some particular theological line which early Christian preachers wanted to promulgate. For Bultmann anything that savoured of the miraculous – the nativity stories, references to angels, accounts of wondrous cures of the sick, and the like – could immediately be dismissed as prompted by the writer's concern to represent Jesus as divine. Anything that appeared to fulfil an Old Testament prophecy – Jesus' birth in Bethlehem, his entry into Jerusalem on a donkey, his betrayal, and much else – could be rejected as a mere attempt to represent his life as fulfilling such prophecies. If anything that Jesus was reported to have said could be traced to the general Jewish thinking of his time, then it was unacceptable as necessarily originating from him. For instance, Jesus' famous saying, '. . . . always treat others as you would like them to treat you; that is the meaning of the Law and the Prophets' (Matthew 7: 12) may be found mirrored almost exactly in a saying of the great Jewish Rabbi Hillel, from less than a century before Jesus: 'Whatever is hateful to you, do not do to your fellow-man. This is the whole Law [Torah] . . .' We cannot therefore be sure that this was ever said by Jesus. Similarly, in Mark's gospel, Jesus is reported as telling a paralytic: 'Your sins are forgiven' (Mark 2: 5). Jewish scribes were then said to have challenged Jesus' right to offer such forgiveness, on the grounds that only God can forgive sins. According to Mark Jesus went on to cure the paralytic regardless. Bultmann argued that this story was probably invented by early Christians to bolster their own claim to be able to forgive sins. By a series of deductions of this kind he concluded that much of what appears in the gospels was not what Jesus had actually said and done, but what Christians at least two generations removed had invented about him, or had inferred from what early preachers had told them. Not surprisingly, Bultmann's approach left intact little that might have derived from the original Jesus – not much more than the parables, Jesus' baptism, his Galilean and Judaean ministries and his crucifixion. Recognizing this himself, he condemned as useless further attempts to try to reconstruct the Jesus of history:

> I do indeed think that we can now know almost nothing concerning the life and personality of Jesus, since the early Christian sources show no interest in either, are moreover fragmentary and often legendary.

Bultmann's recourse was to the Lutheran concept of a Christ of faith, in his view a concept far superior to anything relying on works of history. And he and his colleagues seem to have happily accepted a divine Jesus while rejecting most of the historical evidence for his existence. Dr Geza Vermes, a leading present-day Jewish scholar, has neatly summarized the Bultmann position as having 'their feet off the ground of history and their heads in the clouds of faith'.

Bultmann died in 1976, at the age of ninety-two. A whole generation of modern New Testament scholars, among them his Marburg successor Werner Kümmel, Bristol University's Dennis Nineham, Harvard University's Helmut Koester, and others, acknowledge an immense debt to him for introducing a whole new school of thought in theological research. Others, however, recognize that Bultmann went too far, and have challenged his rigid, unshakable attitudes: in Britain, while acknowledging that each gospel *per se* may have been written at second hand, several scholars have devoted great attention to the detection of underlying first-hand sources. Not long after Bultmann had begun his professorship at Marburg, across the Channel at Queen's College, Oxford, a shy and retiring Englishman, Canon Burnett Streeter, quietly put the finishing touches to *The Four Gospels – A Study in Origins*. By this time, thanks to both British and German theological research, it was already recognized that the authors of Matthew and Luke, in addition to drawing on the gospel of Mark, must have used a second Greek source, long lost, but familiarly referred to by scholars as 'Q' (from the German 'quelle', meaning source). It was even possible to reconstruct Q's original content from passages in which Matthew and Luke bore close resemblance to each other, but not to Mark. While reaffirming this thinking, Streeter postulated at least two additional sources: 'M', which seemed to have provided material peculiar to the Matthew gospel, and 'L' which furnished passages exclusive to Luke. Streeter evolved a chart of the synoptic gospels' possible interrelationship and dependence upon such sources (see over). 'M' and 'L' may well have been written in Aramaic, the spoken language of Jesus and his disciples.

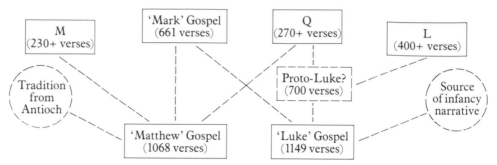

Sources of influence on the synoptic gospels, as deduced by Canon Burnett Streeter. 'Proto-Luke' is a theoretical early gospel, comprising Q plus the special Luke source L, which Streeter believed to have been a prototype for the so-called 'Luke' gospel.

Streeter died in 1937, but his line of thought was developed by other major British theological scholars, among them Professor Charles Dodd, who went on to make his own special contribution to an understanding of the John gospel. To this day the broad outlines of Streeter's hypothesis remain the basis for much synoptic literary criticism. And the clues to underlying Aramaic sources are indeed there. In the Luke gospel, for instance, which includes 'exclusives' such as the parables of the Good Samaritan and the Prodigal Son, there occurs the following saying:

Oh, you Pharisees! You clean the outside of cup and plate, while inside yourselves you are filled with extortion and wickedness ... Instead *give alms* from what you have and then indeed everything will be clean for you. (Luke 11: 39-41).

'Give alms' appears to make no sense, yet it occurs in the very earliest available Greek texts. All becomes clear, however, when we discover that in Aramaic 'zakkau' (to give alms) looks very similar to 'dakkau' (to cleanse). That the original saying referred to 'cleansing' rather than 'giving alms' can be checked because Matthew includes a parallel passage in what we may now judge to have been the correct form: 'Blind Pharisee! Clean the inside of cup and dish first so that the outside may become clean as well ...' (Matthew 23: 26). As has been remarked by Cambridge theologian Don Cupitt, this tells us more clearly than any amount of scholarship that whoever wrote Luke was not inventing his material, but was struggling with an Aramaic source that he was obviously determined to follow even if he did not fully understand it.

A similar misunderstanding is detectable in the Matthew gospel, notable for its remarkable 'Sermon on the Mount' passages, some of which, when translated from Greek into Aramaic, take on such a distinctive verse form that Aramaic must have been the language in which they were first framed. It is like translating the words 'On the bridge at Avignon' back into their original French.

Surprisingly, despite having been dismissed by the Germans as very late and very Greek, the gospel which would seem, in part at least, to have the most authentically Aramaic flavour of all is that of John. The first shock to the nineteenth-century Germans, with their dismissive attitude towards the John gospel, came with the discovery and publication of the Rylands fragment. If a copy of the John gospel was in use in provincial Egypt around 125 AD, its original, if it was composed at Ephesus (and at least no-one has suggested it was written in Egypt), must have been written significantly earlier, probably at least a decade before 100 AD, as most scholars now recognize. A second shock was the discovery of the much publicized Dead Sea Scrolls. Although generally thought to have been written by the Essenes, a Jewish sect contemporary with Jesus, they proved disappointingly to throw little new light on Jesus and early Christianity, at least in any direct way. The Scrolls contain no recognizable mention of Jesus, just as the Christian gospels, surprisingly, fail to refer to the Essenes. But the intriguing feature of the Scrolls is that their authors, undeniably full-blooded Jews, were using in Jesus' time precisely the type of language and imagery previously thought 'Hellenistic' in John. As is well known, the John gospel prologue speaks of a conflict between light and darkness. The whole gospel is replete with phrases such as 'the spirit of truth', 'the light of life', 'walking in the darkness', 'children of light', and 'eternal life'. A welter of such phrases and imagery occur in the Dead Sea Scrolls' Manual of Discipline. The John gospel's prologue,

> He was with God in the beginning.
> Through him all things came to be,
> Not one thing had its being but through him.

(John 1: 2-3)

is strikingly close to the Manual of Discipline's

> All things come to pass by his knowledge,
> He establishes all things by his design
> And without him nothing is done.

(Manual 11: 11)

This is but one example of a striking similarity of cadence and choice of words obvious to anyone reading gospel and Manual side by side.

Left A chance exploration in these caves overlooking the Dead Sea brought to light Jewish documents from close to the time of Jesus, the famous Dead Sea Scrolls. Their phraseology is strikingly similar to that of the gospel of John, which was previously dismissed by the German scholars as late and Hellenistic.

Above Roman flagstones in the crypt of the Sion convent, Jerusalem, which may be the stones referred to in John 19: 13 as the 'Pavement, in Hebrew Gabbatha' where Pilate pronounced sentence on Jesus.

Even before such discoveries Oxford scholar Professor F.C. Burney and ancient historian A.T. Olmstead had begun arguing forcibly that the John gospel's narrative element, at least, must originally have been composed in Aramaic, probably not much later than 40 AD. One ingenious researcher, Dr Aileen Guilding, has shown in *The Fourth Gospel and Jewish Worship* that the gospel's whole construction is based on the Jewish cycle of feasts, and the practice of completing the reading of the Law, or Torah, in a three-year cycle. That the gospel's author incorporated accounts provided by close eyewitnesses to the events described is further indicated by detailed and accurate references to geographical features of Jerusalem and its environs before the city and its Temple were destroyed in 70 AD, after Roman suppression of the Jewish revolt which had broken out four years earlier. It is John who mentions a Pool of Siloam (John 9: 7), remains of which are thought to have been discovered in Jerusalem, and a 'Gabbatha' or pavement, where Pilate is said to have sat in judgement over Jesus (Chapter 19, verse 13). The Gabbatha is identified as a pavement now in the crypt of the Convent of the Sisters of Our Lady of Sion in Jerusalem, undeniably Roman, though not conclusively dating from the time of Jesus.

While some elements in the gospels are clumsily handled and suggest that their authors were far removed in time and distance from the events they are describing, others have a strikingly original and authentic ring. In some instances it is as if a second generation has heavily adulterated first-hand material. Support for such an idea exists, at least in the case of the Matthew gospel, in the form of a cryptic remark by the early Bishop Papias (*c.* 60–130 AD): 'Matthew compiled the *Sayings* in the Aramaic language, and everyone translated them as well as he could.' This has been interpreted as suggesting that all that Matthew might have done was make a collection, in his native Aramaic, of those sayings of Jesus that he had heard, a collection, perhaps in form at least, very like those discovered in the Nag Hammadi Thomas gospel. Someone else, perhaps several others, would then have translated them and adapted them for their own literary purposes. This might readily explain why the Matthew gospel bears his name without, at least in the form it has come down to us, ever having been written by him. The crunch question, though, is why this situation should have come about. Why should original eyewitness material, emanating from Jews who had actually spoken with Jesus and observed his doings, have been adulterated and effectively buried by what were probably Gentile writers of a later time?

The answer appears to lie in one event, the Jewish revolt of 66 AD, which had its culmination four years later in the sacking of Jerusalem, the burning

Carved for perpetuity on Titus' triumphal arch, the victorious army processes through the
streets of Rome with spoils from the Jerusalem Temple, among them the great Temple
Menorah, or seven-branched candelabrum.

of its Temple, and the widespread extermination and humiliation of the Jewish people. As is historically well attested, in 70 AD the Roman general Titus returned in triumph to Rome, parading through the streets such Jewish treasures as the *menorah* (the huge seven-branched candelabrum of the Temple), and enacting tableaux demonstrating how he and his armies had overcome savage, ill-advised resistance from this renegade group of the Empire's subjects, many of whom he had to crucify wholesale. At the height of the celebrations the captured Jewish leader, Simon bar Giora, was dragged to the Forum, abused and executed. In Titus' honour Rome's mints crashed out sestertii with the inscription JUDAEA CAPTA, and within a few years a magnificent triumphal arch was erected next to the Temple of Venus.

Intimately linked to this episode, according to at least one British authority, the late Professor S. G. F. Brandon, was the writing of the key canonical gospel of Mark. Generally recognized as having been written in Rome, according to most present-day thinking it was composed around the time of the Revolt and Titus' triumph, and it displays one overwhelming characteristic, a denigration of Jews and whitewashing of Romans. Whoever wrote Mark portrays Jesus' Jewish disciples as a dull, quarrelsome lot, always jockeying for position, failing to understand Jesus, denying him when they are in trouble (as in the case of Peter), and finally deserting him at the time of his arrest. The entire Jewish establishment, Pharisees, Sadducees, chief priests and scribes, is represented as being out to kill Jesus. Even his own family think him 'out of his mind' and want 'to take charge of him'. By contrast Pilate, the Roman, is portrayed as positively pleading for Jesus' life: 'What harm has he done?' (Mark 15: 14). At the very moment when Jesus, amid Jewish taunts, breathes his last it is a Roman centurion, standing at the foot of the cross, who is represented as the first man in history to recognize Jesus as divine: 'In truth this man was a son of God' (Mark 15: 39).

Given the circumstances of the Jewish revolt and Roman triumph, Mark's motive for portraying matters in this way are not too difficult to understand. For the Rome community of Gentile Christians, who would have been still reeling from the atrocities Nero is reported to have inflicted upon them in 64 AD, it could be seen as embarrassing and humiliating that the very founder of their religion had been a member of this accursed Jewish race, crucified at Roman hands like so many of the recent rebels. How could one hope to win more converts in such a situation? For Mark, and for those who followed him, there could be only one answer: to de-Judaize Jesus by representing him as a reject of, and utterly divorced from, his own people. Similarly, the Luke gospel even avoids representing Roman soldiers as crucifying Jesus,

Pilate, as a Roman, washes his hands of responsibility for Jesus' death. From a sarcophagus in the Lateran Museum, Rome.

Sestertius minted in 70 AD to mark the crushing of the Jewish revolt. A Roman general towers in triumph over a grieving woman, symbolic of the defeated Jewish people. The inscription 'JUDAEA CAPTA' means 'Judaea taken'.

47

and Matthew insists on the Jews' assumption of responsibility for Jesus' death: 'His blood be on us and on our children' (Matthew 27: 25). There is a strikingly anti-Jewish character to the speeches attributed to Jesus in the John gospel too, where Jesus is recorded as condemning 'the Jews' in the most vituperative way. When speaking to them he is quoted as referring to 'your Law', i.e. the Torah, as if this was no part of his own beliefs, and telling them that they are uncompromisingly evil, with the Devil as their father (John 8: 43–7).

According to at least one interpretation of events, the Jewish revolt therefore needs to be seen as a vital key to an understanding of how and when the canonical gospels came to be written. Because of the manuscript discoveries, it is now generally accepted that the gospels cannot have been written as late as the nineteenth-century German theologians supposed. Among many other considerations, one of the factors which has influenced the dating proposed by Werner Kümmel (see below) is the inclusion in the gospels of apparent prophecies by Jesus of the fall of Jerusalem and destruction of the Temple (Matthew 24: 1–3; Mark 13: 1–4; Luke 21: 5–7), and the parable of the wedding feast (Matthew 22: 1–10; Luke 14: 16–24). In line with Bultmann's thinking, these are interpreted as prophecies written after the event, a substantial body of present-day theologians having adopted this viewpoint.

But such a line of argument is by no means universally accepted, and in 1976 Dr John Robinson, then Dean of Chapel at Trinity College, Cambridge, well known for his controversial *Honest to God*, offered an entirely new approach in *Redating the New Testament*. Here he expressed surprise

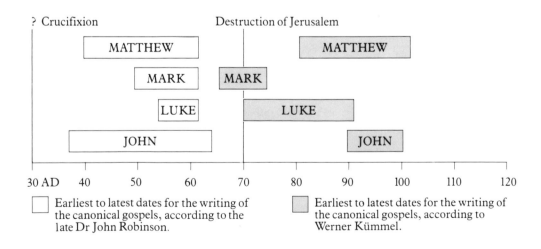

that if the gospels were not written until after Jerusalem's fall, the writers should not have pointedly capitalized on the obvious fulfilment of Jesus' prophecies. The revolt as a past event goes entirely unmentioned. Among indications that the gospels originated before 70 AD, Dr Robinson pointed to the Matthew gospel reference to the Jews' obligation to pay the Temple tax (Matthew 17: 24-27), a burden which disappeared after the Temple's destruction. If the gospels were written after 70 AD, why should their writers have represented Jesus as predicting his return 'before this generation has passed away' (Matthew 24: 34-36; Mark 13: 30-32; Luke 21: 32-33), a prediction which would have been a little late for anyone living in the generation after the Jewish revolt? Dr Robinson's arguments are not accepted by any consensus of New Testament scholars, and are in conflict, for instance, with the insights of Professor Brandon. But at the very least they add force to the argument that some elements of all the gospels are of very early origin, even if they have been re-edited.

It is clear that the canonical gospels are neither the second-century tissue of fabrications argued by Strauss and others, nor quite the contemporary eyewitness descriptions that, given the nature of Christianity's claims, we might not unreasonably expect. Ironically, it has not been theologians but outsiders, such as scholars of ancient history, well used to imperfections in the works of the pagan writers of antiquity, who have been most prepared to recognize the strong vein of authenticity underlying the gospels. As argued by Nicholas Sherwin-White in *Roman Society and Roman Law in the New Testament*:

... it can be maintained that those who had a passionate interest in the story of Christ, even if their interest in events was parabolical and didactic rather than historical, would not be led by that very fact to pervert and utterly destroy the historical kernel of their material.

Sherwin-White's view has been echoed by the Oxford English don C. S. Lewis, speaking particularly of the John gospel:

I have been reading poems, romances, vision literature, legends, myths all my life. I know what they are like. I know that none of them is like this. Of this text there are only two possible views. Either this is reportage - though it may no doubt contain errors - pretty close to the facts; nearly as close as Boswell. Or else, some unknown writer in the second century, without known predecessors or successors, suddenly anticipated the whole technique of modern, novelistic, realistic narrative. If it is untrue, it must be narrative of that kind. The reader who doesn't see this simply has not learned to read.

So how are we to judge the gospels? Because of the claims they make, because they were written at least a generation after the lifetime of their principal subject, and because they have suffered much distortion, it is important that we take nothing for granted – not least that Jesus of Nazareth even existed.

DID JESUS EVEN EXIST?

IT may appear self-evident that Jesus once existed as a human being, but there have been and continue to be many who would deny this. In the Soviet Union it is a basic part of Communist education that Jesus was invented in the second century AD to account for an early proletarian communist movement. In 1970 Manchester University oriental studies specialist John Allegro, in *The Sacred Mushroom and the Cross*, argued in all seriousness that Christianity began as a secret cult of the sacred mushroom, and that the name 'Jesus' was a code-word for this. Recently the most enthusiastic and plausible exponent, in Britain at least, of the theory that Jesus did not exist has been G.A. Wells, professor of German at Birkbeck College, London. Although outside his specialist field, during the last twelve years Wells has produced no fewer than three scholarly books on the subject, the latest being *The Historical Evidence for Jesus*, essentially arguing that the Jesus of the gospels did not exist.

According to Wells, the writings of the apostle Paul form the linchpin of his argument. Wells acknowledges that Paul existed, and also that the historical Paul wrote at least some of the New Testament letters attributed to him that, it is generally agreed, predate the canonical gospels. The real interest of these letters for Wells lies in their apparent ignorance of any details of Jesus' earthly life. Paul does not name Jesus' parents, where he was born, where he lived, even when he lived. Although his writings comprise a substantial proportion of the New Testament, they contain no mention of Jesus' parables or 'miracles' (Paul seems even to deny that Jesus worked any miracles), no reference to his trial before Pilate, nor of Jerusalem as the place of his execution. This is undeniably a striking feature of Paul's writings. On his own admission, Paul never knew the human Jesus, and based his whole faith on a vision he claimed to have received of the resurrected Jesus, a fact that was to have profound consequences for the whole character of later Christianity, as will be shown later in this book.

For centuries Christians have imagined Jesus' birth to have been in the stable of an inn, surrounded by farm animals, but this conception does not derive from the gospels. The Greek text of Luke speaks of a *katalemna*, a temporary shelter, or even a cave; a very early Christian tradition also locates Jesus' birth in a cave; and it was over a cave that the Emperor Constantine built Bethlehem's Church of the Nativity. Similarly the Greek word *thaten*, which appears as 'manger' in most bible translations, simply means 'crib' when used in connection with a baby. The popular concept may well have been inspired by the Old Testament passage 'The ox knows its owner, and the ass its master's crib' (Isaiah 1: 3), as in this early nativity representation on a sarcophagus in the Christian lapidarium at Arles.

Opposite, *top* A Roman census, first century BC. By suggesting that Jesus was born at the time of Quirinius, the author of the Luke gospel appears to offer an impressive piece of historical detail. But Quirinius' census took place in 6 AD, incompatible with the information in Matthew 2: 1 that Jesus' birth was during the reign of King Herod, who died in 4 BC. Detail from the so-called Altar of Domitius Ahenobarbus, Louvre, Paris.

John Kepler (1571–1630), astronomer to the court of Prague, and his 'Star of Bethlehem' theory. Observing an unusual conjunction of planets in 1603, Kepler calculated that a similar conjunction would have occurred in 7 BC, explaining the so-called 'Star of Bethlehem'. An alternative theory is that the star may have been a nova, but the Matthew author may have simply invented the story, perhaps inspired by Balaam's 'star from Jacob' of Numbers 24: 17.

For Wells the inescapable deduction to be drawn from this situation was that Jesus was a figment of Paul's imagination. When people began to believe in this imaginary figure, he had to be given a historical setting in a specific place and time. Constructing the background became the work of the gospel writers, who drew on all sorts of Old Testament material to give flesh to the figure, finally fabricating an execution during the known Roman governorship of Pontius Pilate.

Horrifying as Wells' views might appear to many Christians, it has to be acknowledged that hard facts concerning Jesus and his life are remarkably hard to come by. Not even the gospels give us the smallest crumb of information about what he looked like – whether he was tall or short, bearded or clean shaven, handsome or ugly. As required by the Hebrew scriptures (Exodus 20: 4), portraiture was shunned by most practising Jews of Jesus' time, as a result of which the earliest known depictions of him are Gentile works dating from the third century onwards. These exhibit such striking variations, most depicting him as beardless (whereas, as a Jew, he would almost certainly have worn a beard), that it is obvious that even at such an early time any authoritative idea of what he looked like had already been lost. Of the details of Jesus' life, Canon Streeter, mentioned in the previous chapter, once calculated that, with the exception of the forty days and nights in the wildnerness (of which we are told virtually nothing), everything described in the gospels could be compressed into three weeks, which leaves by far the greater part of Jesus' life unrecorded.

However punctiliously Christians celebrate Jesus' birth each 25 December, not only the date but also the year of his birth are unknown, and on present evidence, unknowable. Neither Mark's gospel, apparently the earliest of the three synoptics, nor John's give any account of the circumstances of Jesus' birth. In the two gospels which do, Matthew's and Luke's, the nativity stories contradict each other in some important particulars, and offer little which inspires confidence. The historian and writer Marina Warner, in her recent study *Alone of All Her Sex – the Myth and Cult of the Virgin Mary*, has produced an excellent, yet inevitably disquieting summary of the main areas of uncertainty and conflict. For instance, according to Matthew's gospel the news of Jesus' impending birth is conveyed to Mary's husband Joseph in a dream, while according to Luke it is conveyed directly to Mary by the 'Angel Gabriel'. According to Luke, Jesus' parents had to travel from their home in Nazareth to Bethlehem for the Roman census, while according to Matthew they lived in Bethlehem already, and were only obliged to leave when, in an incident which has no historical corroboration,

King Herod began killing off the children. Although in Luke Jesus is represented as God's son by Mary, his ancestry is illogically traced back to King David via his human father Joseph. While Matthew's gospel similarly gives Jesus' genealogy via the male line, it provides a list of antecedents so different from those in Luke that even Joseph's father appears with a different name – Jacob instead of Heli.

And these are by no means the greatest weaknesses of the Matthew and Luke nativity stories. Matthew tries to justify Jesus' apparently divine parentage from Isaiah's famous prophecy: 'The virgin will conceive and give birth to a son' (Isaiah 7: 14). Yet this all too clearly reveals that whoever wrote at least this part of Matthew's gospel was no true Jew. In the original Hebrew text of Isaiah the crucial word *'almah* is used, which simply means 'young woman'. It carries a general connotation of eligibility for marriage, but not necessarily of virginity. Only when, in the third century BC, the Hebrew scriptures were translated into Greek, to become the Septuagint – the bible of those Jews so absorbed into Greek-speaking communities that they had lost much of their Hebrew – was the Greek word *parthenos* inaccurately used as a translation of *'almah*, carrying with it a strong implication of untouched virginity unintended in the original Hebrew. To this day, no true Jew expects the Messiah of Isaiah's prophecy, whoever he may be, and whenever he may appear, to be conceived by anything other than normal human means. The Luke nativity narrative stands up no better to careful scrutiny. Mary's famous *Magnificat* (Luke 1: 46–55) is all too obviously based on the song of Hannah in 1 Samuel 2: 1–10. And after telling us that the announcements of the births of Jesus and John the Baptist took place in the reign of Herod the Great, who is known to have died in 4 BC, the Luke author tries to offer a piece of impressive historical detail:

> Now at this time Caesar Augustus issued a decree for a census of the whole world to be taken. This census – the first – took place while Quirinius was governor of Syria, and everyone went to his home town to be registered ... (Luke 2: 1–3)

Unfortunately, while the first-ever census among Jews did indeed take place during Quirinius' governorship, this did not and could not have happened until at least 6 AD, the first year that Judaea came under direct Roman rule, and it was reliably recorded by Josephus as an unprecedented event of that year. To put it bluntly, Luke has resorted to invention.

In this light the credibility of the Matthew and Luke nativity narratives must be acknowledged to be doubtful. The nativity stories, in any case, sit somewhat uncomfortably in the gospels' opening chapters, and are never referred to again. This makes it difficult to take seriously attempts to date Jesus' birth by Matthew's references (Matthew 2: 2–11) to an unusual star which hung over Bethlehem at the time. On 17 December 1603 the Tübingen-educated German astronomer John Kepler observed a striking conjunction of the planets Saturn and Jupiter in the constellation Pisces, and calculated that a similar conjunction must have occurred in 7 BC. He speculated that this might have been the true year of Jesus' birth, it generally being agreed that the original dating of the nativity to the year 1 AD, by the sixth-century monk Dionysius Exiguus, derived from a miscalculation. Kepler found support for his theory in a Jewish rabbinical reference to the Messiah appearing when Saturn and Jupiter were in conjunction in the constellation of Pisces. Seventy-nine years later English astronomer Edmund Halley discovered the comet that now bears his name. It was calculated that one of its periodic fly-pasts would have occurred in 12 BC, and this in its turn gave credence to the idea that Halley's comet might have been the star of Bethlehem. Much more recently three British astronomers, David Clark of the Royal Greenwich Observatory, John Parkinson of Dorking's Mullard Space Science Laboratory, and Richard Stephenson of Newcastle University, have offered yet another theory – that the star of Bethlehem was a nova, or exploding star, visible to Chinese astronomers of the Han dynasty 'for more than seventy days' in 5 BC. Intriguing as all such speculations are, it has to be admitted that the true date of Jesus' birth is unknown.

A similar uncertainty surrounds the date of Jesus' death, again because of gospel contradictions. According to the authors of the four canonical gospels, and also to the Roman historian Tacitus, Jesus' death occurred during the governorship of Judaea by Pontius Pilate, whose term of administration is known to have been between 27 and 36 AD. Confusion breaks out, however, when we learn from the three synoptic gospels that Jesus' Last Supper was a Passover Meal (Matthew 26: 17–20; Mark 14: 12–17; Luke 22: 7–14), while according to John it was the day of the crucifixion itself that was 'Passover Preparation Day' (John 19: 14). This is an important factor in calculating the year of Jesus' death, because the Passover always falls on 15 Nisan (Nisan roughly corresponds to our April), and all gospels are agreed that the day immediately after the crucifixion was a Sabbath. Because of the gospel discrepancies, however, we cannot be sure whether we are looking for a year in which 14 Nissan fell on a Thursday or a Friday. Ingenious attempts have been made to reconcile the differences by suggesting that Jesus and his disciples, along with the Essenes of the Dead Sea Scrolls, may have celebrated the Passover according to an ancient solar calendar different from

Above Claudius (41–54 AD) *Right* Nero (54–68 AD)
Writing of the reign of Claudius, the early second-century writer Suetonius described Jews of Rome rebelling at the instigation of 'Chrestus'. Almost contemporary with Suetonius, the Roman historian Tacitus wrote of Rome's Christians being blamed by Nero for the city's great fire. Tacitus remarked that the Christians' founder, 'Christ', had been executed by Pontius Pilate, whom he anachronistically referred to as 'procurator'. Both historians were clearly somewhat distant from the original events.

that observed by the Jews of Jerusalem. Another possibility is that Mark, as the first of the synoptics, simply got his facts wrong, and that the authors of Matthew and Luke, because they copied from Mark, made the same error. Yet another possibility is that John, in a desire to represent Jesus as the new 'paschal lamb', artificially fixed the moment of crucifixion as coinciding with the time when lambs would have been slaughtered in the Jerusalem Temple in preparation for the Passover.

An independent means of dating the crucifixion is offered by the fact that Luke dates Jesus' baptism by John the Baptist to the fifteenth year of the reign of the Emperor Tiberius, calculable as 29 AD. The synoptic gospels suggest that Jesus' public ministry lasted no longer than a year, placing the crucifixion in 30 AD. But the John gospel again complicates the picture by suggesting that Jesus' ministry spanned some three years after his baptism, leading one school of thought to set the date of the crucifixion as 33 AD. The likeliest dates have been calculated to be 30, 33 and 27 AD, in that order of probability, but Schonfield, author of the famous *Passover Plot*, places it in 36 AD. Again the only honest conclusion is that we simply do not know the exact year when Jesus died.

All this uncertainty may lend some credence to the arguments of Professor Wells, that Jesus was merely an invention of the gospel writers. At first sight this appears to be borne out by the lack of references to Jesus outside the gospels. Although, as already noted, the great Roman historian Tacitus mentioned Jesus, close scrutiny reveals that his reference is not very clear or specific. Tacitus spoke merely of certain Christians, barbarically put to death on Nero's orders, whose 'originator, Christ, had been executed in Tiberius' reign by the governor of Judaea, Pontius Pilate.'

Wells can justifiably argue that a totally illusory belief that Jesus was a historical figure might have grown up by the time that Tacitus was writing, in the second century. His remoteness from contemporary records is indicated by his reference to Jesus as 'Christ', as if this was his proper name, whereas in fact it is merely a Greek form of the Hebrew *Māshīah* (Messiah), or 'anointed one'. Tacitus' near contemporary Suetonius was apparently no better informed. He refers merely to some Jews of Rome who, during the reign of Claudius (41–54 AD), rebelled at the instigation of one 'Chrestus'. The only other early classical reference is that of Pliny the Younger, who, as a rather fussy governor of Bithynia, wrote to Trajan in 112 AD reporting Christians to be an apparently harmless people who met at daybreak and sang hymns to their Messiah. Pliny commented of them, 'I could discover nothing more than a depraved and excessive superstition.' In all

Flavius Josephus (*c*.37–100 AD), whose prolific writings provide the main source of information on Jewish history of the first century AD. Although his reference to Jesus has undeniably suffered from Christian adulteration, Josephus evidently knew of Jesus, thereby confirming his existence. Roman bust, Ny Carlsberg Glypotek, Copenhagen.

this there is scarcely a crumb of information to compel a belief in Jesus' existence.

But where we meet evidence of an altogether different order is in the writings of the Jewish historian Josephus. Born in 37 or 38 AD, the son of a Judaean priest, Josephus was educated as a Pharisee. In 66 AD he helped defend Galilee against the Romans during the Jewish revolt, but when captured took the bitterly resented step of defecting to the Romans, subsequently pleading with his countrymen that resistance was useless. In 70 AD, after acting as Titus' interpreter during the siege of Jerusalem, he moved to Rome, and was well looked after by successive Roman Emperors. As a result of their patronage he had the leisure to write *The Jewish War*, which he completed around 77 or 78 AD, followed about fifteen years later by his monumental *The Antiquities of the Jews*. These two works represent our prime surviving sources of information on the history of the Jewish people during the first century of the Christian era.

An important feature of Josephus' writings is their high degree of detail, and where they can be checked from archaeology, as for instance in the case of their description of the fall of Masada, they are impressively accurate. Masada's excavation even revealed inscribed potsherds used in the casting of lots before the defenders' dramatic suicide, as Josephus described. It is also quite clear that Josephus, although certainly not a Christian, was interested in matters of religion: in his early life he spent three years in the desert with a religious hermit called Bannos. We would therefore expect him to make some mention of a historical Jesus and his followers, and indeed he appears to do so, in the *Antiquities*:

At about this time lived Jesus, a wise man, if indeed one might call him a man. For he was one who accomplished surprising feats and was a teacher of such people as are eager for novelties. He won over many of the Jews and many of the Greeks. He was the Messiah. When Pilate, upon an indictment brought by the principal men among us, condemned him to the cross, those who had loved him from the very first did not cease to be attached to him. On the third day he appeared to them restored to life, for the holy prophets had foretold this and myriads of other marvels concerning him. And the tribe of the Christians, so called after him, has to this day still not disappeared.

Since Josephus was, judging by the rest of his writings, quite obviously not a Christian, Professor Wells is convinced that this passage was the interpolation of a later Christian copyist. That someone has certainly adulterated the passage, very clumsily, in a pro-Christian way has long been undeniable. But is it a complete invention? It so happens that there occurs later in

Josephus' *Antiquities* a reference to the unjust execution in 62 AD of James 'the brother of Jesus called the Christ'. Professor Wells has dismissed this too as just another interpolation. But it does not sound like one, for the simple reason that it refers to Jesus merely as 'called the Christ', inconsistent with the earlier passage, and just the sort of remark Josephus might well have made, given his religious standpoint. Furthermore, we know that this passage existed in a very early version of his text, together with a passage casting doubt on Jesus' Messiahship. In the third century AD the Christian writer Origen had expressed his astonishment that Josephus, while disbelieving that Jesus was the Messiah, should have spoken so warmly about his brother. This information from Origen is incontrovertible evidence that Josephus referred to Jesus before any Christian copyist would have had a chance to make alterations.

Returning to the quoted passage from *Antiquities*, perhaps it was, after all, written by Josephus and merely adulterated with a pro-Christian gloss. An indication that this may be so is to be found in the opening description of Jesus as 'a wise man', a comment quite untypical of any Christian writer but characteristic of Josephus. Jewish scholars such as Dr Geza Vermes have tried removing all pro-Christian elements from the passage, recovering what they believe to be at least an approximation, if incomplete, of what Josephus originally wrote:

At about this time lived Jesus, a wise man ... He performed astonishing feats (and was a teacher of such people as are eager for novelties?) He attracted many Jews and many of the Greeks ... Upon an indictment brought by leading members of our society, Pilate sentenced him to the cross, but those who had loved him from the very first did not cease to be attached to him ... The brotherhood of the Christians, named after him, is still in existence ...

There is excellent justification for such a restoration. The words 'astonishing feats', or more literally 'paradoxical deeds', are precisely the same as those used by Josephus to describe the healings of Elisha. The reconstructed text corresponds closely with a possibly unadulterated version preserved in the writings of the tenth-century Arabic Christian Agapius, which also includes the following:

... his disciples ... reported that he had appeared to them three days after his crucifixion and that he was alive; accordingly he was perhaps the Messiah, concerning whom the prophets have recounted wonders.

If Josephus originally wrote something approximating to these words, and Jewish as well as Christian scholars have been prepared to affirm that he did, then we have positive and authoritative confirmation of Jesus' existence from very nearly the best possible independent source, a man who actually lived in Galilee well within the lifetimes of individuals who would have known Jesus at first hand.

Other early Jewish sources too, while similarly saying nothing very favourable about Jesus, at least tacitly acknowledge that he existed. Among both Christians and Jews these references are all too little known because, as a result of Christian persecution, Jewish religious books came under repeated attack during the Middle Ages, and references of all kinds were censored and not restored. But the last two generations of Jewish scholars, anxious to discover who Jesus was, have done much to retrieve them.

For the benefit of the non-Jewish reader it should be explained that the Talmud, that is the collection of Jewish religious literature compiled since the writing of the Old Testament, comprises the *Mishnah*, which consists of rabbinic writings up to about 200 AD, and the *Gemara*, a commentary on the *Mishnah*, completed between the third and fifth centuries. Because of its earlier date it is the *Mishnah* that is most relevant to the life of Jesus; although it does not itself make direct reference to him, its supplements, the *Baraitha* and *Tosefta*, both equally early, do so at least five times. In each instance, according to American Rabbi Morris Goldstein and others, the man referred to may be confidently identified with the Jesus of Christianity. The following are some examples:

1 It has been taught: On the eve of Passover they hanged Yeshu . . . because he practised sorcery and enticed and led Israel astray . . .

2 Our rabbis taught: Yeshu had five disciples – Mattai, Nakkai, Netzer, Buni and Todah.

3 It happened with Rabbi Elazar ben Damah, whom a serpent bit, that Jacob, a man of Kefar Soma, came to heal him in the name of Yeshu[a] ben Pantera; but Rabbi Ishmael did not let him. He said 'You are not permitted, Ben Damah'. He answered, 'I will bring you proof that he may heal me.' But he had no opportunity to bring proof, for he died.

4 Once, I was walking on the upper street of Sepphoris [capital of Galilee], and found one of the disciples of Yeshu the Nazarene, by the name Jacob, a man of Kefar Sechanya. He said to me, 'It is written in your Torah: "Thou shalt not bring the hire of a harlot, etc." How about making with it a privy for the high priest?' But I did not answer him at all. He told me, 'Thus did Yeshu the Nazarene teach me: "For the hire of a harlot hath she gathered them, And unto the hire of a harlot shall they return", from the place of filth

Jesus' real father? According to one widespread early Jewish story, Jesus was the illegitimate son of a Roman soldier called Pantera or Panthera. The name is an unusual one, and was thought to be an invention until this first-century tombstone came to light in Bingerbrück, Germany. The inscription reads: 'Tiberius Julius Abdes Pantera of Sidon, aged 62, a soldier of 40 years' service, of the 1st cohort of archers, lies here.' Bad Kreuznach Museum, W. Germany they come, and unto the place of filth they shall go.' And the utterance pleased me ...

Despite the puzzling number and names of the disciples, the other information, such as the hanging of 'Yeshu' on the eve of the Passover (incidentally corroborating the John gospel chronology), the specific appellation 'Yeshu the Nazarene', his association with Galilee, and his accrediting with healings and 'sorcery', indicates beyond reasonable doubt that this Yeshu was one and the same as the Jesus of the gospels. 'Jesus' is, in fact, the usual Graeco-Roman adaptation of the Semitic 'Yeshu'. The 'ben Pantera' (meaning 'son of Pantera') patronym used in the third example crops up repeatedly in later Jewish references, which were more scurrilous than those of the earlier, Tannaitic period. They claim Jesus/Yeshu to have been the son of an illegitimate union between his mother Miriam, or Mary, and a Roman soldier variously called Pandera, Pantera or Panthera. That a rumour of this kind, whether or not it was soundly based, was at least early in origin is incontrovertible because the Christian writer Origen tells us that he heard about it from the second-century pagan philosopher Celsus. Celsus in his turn claimed to have heard it from a Jew, so the story seems to have been in circulation around 150 AD. Christian writers have tended to dismiss this story as a malicious piece of invention, suggesting that 'Panthera' may have been a corruption of 'parthenos' or virgin. Intriguingly their interpretation fell a little flat with the discovery at Bingerbrück in Germany of the tombstone of one Tiberius Julius Abdes Panthera, a Roman archer from Sidon in Phoenicia. Although it would be fanciful seriously to suggest that Panthera was Jesus' real father, the tombstone does happen to date from the appropriate early Roman Imperial period.

In this same connection, a peculiarity of the genealogy ascribed to Jesus in the Matthew gospel is that the only four female ancestors named – Tamar, Rahab, Ruth and Bathsheba – each happen to have been 'fallen women'. Tamar was a temple prostitute; Rahab was the madam of a brothel; Ruth, the most moral, indulged in some pretty shameless sexual exploitation; and Bathsheba committed adultery with King David. Was the author of the Matthew genealogy implying something about the only other woman mentioned, Mary herself? From the Christian viewpoint it is of course possible to interpret the same evidence quite differently, as confirmation that there was something strange and supernatural about the circumstances surrounding Jesus' paternity.

The true corollary, however, is that had Jesus been a mere fabrication by early Christians, we should surely expect those Jews hostile to Christianity to have produced a malicious rumour to this effect. From the fact that they concentrated instead on smearing his legitimacy, we may deduce that they had no grounds whatever for doubting his historical existence. In opposition to Professor Wells' deductions that Jesus was a figment of the apostle Paul's imagination, it may be argued that Paul had very good reasons for ignoring most factual details about Jesus' earthly life. Although directly contemporary with many of the apostles, he suffered from the considerable disadvantage of never having known the human Jesus, and he was not one to embark on a retrospective study of Jesus' life (as will be more fully explored later). To have had an experience of the resurrected Jesus was everything he needed, and it is therefore scarcely surprising that *his* Jesus, as distinct from the one of the gospels, should seem ephemeral and unconvincing.

On the most rational grounds, therefore, we may be confident that Professor Wells is wrong, and that Jesus did indeed exist.

JESUS THE JEW

SOME uncontentious background details about Jesus may now be allowed to fall into place. We can accept that he was the son of a Jewish mother. We can also accept, therefore, even without the Luke gospel telling us so (Luke 2:21), that in accordance with the Jewish Law, or Torah, he would have been circumcised on the eighth day after his birth. We can assume that as a Jew Jesus would have had a good education, possibly even from Pharisees, who were the teachers of the ordinary people of the time, although we would not expect to find them in Galilee. For the practice of his religion he would have learned Hebrew, the original Jewish language in which the sacred scriptures were written. As his everyday tongue he would have spoken Aramaic, and it is in that language that certain special utterances he made are quoted untranslated in the Christian gospels.

What of Jesus' name? In deference to the John Allegro 'sacred mushroom' theory, is there any justification for believing it to have had some special significance? In fact, its most striking feature is its utter ordinariness. In Josephus' *Antiquities*, of the twenty-eight high priests who held office from the reign of Herod the Great to the fall of the Temple, no fewer than four bore the name of Jesus: Jesus son of Phiabi, Jesus son of Sec, Jesus son of Damneus and Jesus son of Gamaliel. Several other Jesuses also occur in Josephus' texts, among them a general of Idumaea, a priest's son, and 'the captain of those robbers who were in the confines of Ptolemais'. 'Yeshu', as Jesus would actually have been addressed, means 'God Saves', and is merely a shortened form of the more old fashioned 'Yehoshua' ('Joshua' of the Old Testament). In the first century AD it would have been an extremely common name.

More problematic is the appellation 'the Nazarene' which is linked with Jesus' name both in the gospels and, as already noted, in the Jewish record. Where it occurs in the latter it takes the form 'Hanotzri', not particularly meaningful even to Jews. As Rabbi Morris Goldstein commented:

'It might refer to *netzer*, as in Isaiah 11:1, to mean 'a branch', used in Christian tradition with a messianic connotation. It might allude to Jesus as the source of the Nazarene sect. It might be a derivation from *noter*, which would describe those who *keep* the [new] Law of Jesus. It might mean, as is generally understood, 'of Nazareth'.

For Christians, brought up on the gospel stories, it might seem obvious that 'Nazarene' should mean 'of Nazareth'. Yet this is not necessarily the case. Although modern New Testament translations contain repeated references to 'Jesus of Nazareth', 'Jesus the Nazarene' is the more common form of words in the original Greek version. And one problem rarely appreciated by Christians is that, according to one school of thought, Nazareth may not even have existed in the first century AD. The historian Josephus, in command of Galilee during the Jewish revolt, lists in his writings what appear to be all the region's main towns and villages, but he makes no mention of Nazareth. The earliest the name appears in Jewish literature is in a poem of about the seventh century AD.

However, what appear to be pre-Christian remains were found in 1955 under the Church of the Annunciation in the present-day town of Nazareth. These suggest that the site was occupied in the first century AD. And in 1962 at Caesarea, where the first-century Romans had their administrative headquarters, archaeologists discovered a fragmentary third- to fourth-century inscription incorporating the name 'Nazareth', which probably formed part of a marble tablet displayed on a synagogue wall. Such findings suggest that Nazareth may have existed in Jesus' time, but there is no doubt that it must have been a very small and insignificant place.

The second site associated with Jesus' early years, Capernaum, features rather more decisively in the gospels. For instance, Matthew's gospel describes Jesus as going to live there after leaving Nazareth (Matthew 4:13). John's gospel describes Jesus' disciples as setting out to row to Capernaum as if returning home, after the feeding of the five thousand (John 6:15). Jesus seems to have had a house of sufficient size there to accommodate a large gathering of disciples, tax collectors and sinners (Mark 2:15). He is represented as teaching in the Capernaum synagogue (Mark 1:21). In ancient non-Christian literature Capernaum is almost as inconspicuous as Nazareth, but it does appear once in Josephus' writings, as a 'spring with great fertilising power, known locally as Capharnaum'. Josephus locates it in the highly fertile Gennesaret region on the shores of the Sea of Galilee, and stresses the agricultural abundance of the whole of Galilee:

... excellent for crops or cattle and rich in forests of every kind, so that by its adaptability it invites even those least inclined to work on the land. Consequently

The earliest known reference to Nazareth: a reconstruction from fragments of a grey marble tablet discovered in 1962 during excavations at Caesarea. The original tablet was probably displayed on the wall of a late third- or early fourth-century synagogue, and listed the places where priestly families had settled.

Left Capernaum: remains of an early Jewish synagogue. Although this synagogue dates from no earlier than the late second century, it may well have been built on the site of the one in which Jesus taught (Mark 1: 21).

Galilee. An exceptionally fertile region in the first century AD, it remains so to this day. A striking feature of Jesus' recorded teachings is his rural imagery.

every inch has been cultivated by the inhabitants and not a corner goes to waste . . .

As a Jew from a small village in such a region, Jesus might be expected to have known a great deal about the countryside. And in fact, when the sayings attributed to him in the gospels are examined for background information, they reveal above all a familiarity with country life. Within one chapter of the Luke gospel (Luke 13) Jesus is depicted as knowing how to revive a barren fig tree (vv. 6–9), sensitive to farm animals' need for watering (v. 15), aware of the remarkable growth propensity of mustard seed (v. 19), well informed on the amount of yeast needed to leaven dough (v. 21), and keenly observant of the characteristic manner in which a hen 'gathers her brood under her wings' (v. 34). In the Matthew gospel he is the first man to go on record as interpreting a red sky at night as a portent for good weather the following day (Matthew 16: 1–3). As has been pointed out by Dr Geza Vermes, it is surely significant that Galilee's larger towns – the capital, Sepphoris, only four miles from Nazareth, and Tarichaeae, Garaba and others – go totally unmentioned in the gospels.

As a true countryman of Galilee it is likely that Jesus spoke with the notorious local accent. From sources quite independent of the New Testament, it is known that Galileans caused great amusement to the snobbish southerners of Jesusalem by their characteristic sloppiness in pronouncing Aramaic. The Talmud describes the ridiculing of a Galilean in the Jerusalem market-place for trying to buy what he called *amar*. He was chided: 'You stupid Galilean, do you want something to ride on [*haṁar:* a donkey]? Or something to drink [*hamár:* wine]? Or something for clothing [*'amar:* wool]? Or something for a sacrifice [*immar*: a lamb]?' The Galileans evidently dropped their aitches, or more accurately, their alephs. The Matthew gospel mentions that Jesus' disciple Peter was specifically remarked upon in Jerusalem because of his accent: 'You are one of them for sure! Why your accent gives you away' (Matthew 26:73).

The Galilee connection is supported by references in the gospels to two separate individuals known as Lazarus, one the poor man of Luke 16: 19–31, the other the man raised from the dead, John 11: 1–44. In Jerusalem, as is known from inscriptions on ossuaries (the stone boxes used for gathering the bones of the dead), the name took the form 'Eleazar' or 'Elazar', with the initial *aleph*. But in the Galilean necropolis of Beth She'arim, the name occurs truncated, as 'Lazar' or 'Laze', like the 'Lazarus' of the gospels. Despite being written in Greek, therefore, the gospels convey something of the original Galilean flavour of Jesus and his closest associates.

So, Jesus was probably a Galilean from Nazareth – but what do we really know of his ancestry? He was further removed in time from the original Jewish King David than we are from William the Conqueror, and his lineage is inevitably conjectural. However, one of the very few snippets of information about Jesus provided by the apostle Paul concerns his descent from David (Romans 1:3). And according to the fourth-century church historian Eusebius, who had access to earlier sources, close relations of Jesus were arrested by the Roman authorities for their descent from David for up to a century after the crucifixion.

The gospels make no mention of Jesus' father after the time when Jesus began his teaching, suggesting that by then Joseph was dead. It seems that Jesus then became the head of the family as the eldest of several brothers and sisters (Matthew 13: 55–56; Mark 6: 3), and that the later Jewish illegitimacy slurs should not therefore be treated too seriously. Had Jesus been known to have been illegitimate, we might have expected his eldest legitimate brother to have taken charge of family affairs, but the Mark gospel (3: 31–35), implies that it was to Jesus that his mother, brothers and sisters turned for leadership. It may well be a myth, for which the gospels are not to be blamed, that Jesus' family background was necessarily very poor. There is uncertainty in the Matthew and Mark texts as to whether Jesus was himself a carpenter (Mark 6: 3), or merely a carpenter's son (Matthew 13: 55; Mark 6: 3 variant texts) but, whichever was the case, the term carpenter in New Testament times would have meant something nearer to our 'builder' today. Just as the imagery of a countryman is present in Jesus' sayings, so too is that of a carpenter or builder, for instance in the 'mote' passage already mentioned, which is quoted here in the more modern Jerusalem translation: 'Why do you observe the splinter in your brother's eye and never notice the plank in your own' (Matthew 7: 3–5; Luke 6: 41), and in his saying concerning the house built on rock (Luke 6: 47–49), and his fondness for the words from Psalm 118: 'It was the stone rejected by the builders that became the keystone' (Luke 20: 17 and elsewhere).

That Jesus' experience of life was wider than might be expected of a minor artisan is suggested by the keenly observed cast of characters which populate his parables – the unscrupulous judge, the importunate widow, the crafty steward, the virtuous Pharisee, and so on. These are not stereotyped figures; they carry the conviction that they, or someone like them, had come within Jesus' direct experience.

Assuming that we are dealing with such a keenly observant, country-loving craftsman, let us examine his motives for involving himself in matters of religion. To understand them we need to understand something of the whole underlying character of the Jewish people, their intensely troubled history, and their equally intense relationship with their God.

Though the exact details are lost in the mists of antiquity, we know that when some of Jesus' ancestors had been enslaved in pagan Egypt, probably around the middle of the second millennium BC, it had been an essentially ordinary man – certainly not one with pretensions as king, general or high priest – who, under the name of Moses, appeared from nowhere to lead the Jewish people to freedom. As represented in the biblical record, Moses' action was prompted by what he believed to be the voice of God within him. And what a God! While all around, nations as sophisticated as the Egyptians, Babylonians and Minoans were worshipping what to all appearances were mere idols of wood and stone (sometimes offering them human sacrifices), prostrating themselves before despotic human rulers, and indulging in orgiastic rites to encourage the fertility of their crops, how different were the Jews. Perhaps precisely because of their humble, nomadic origins, their God was unseen and universal. As with the patriarch Abraham, still further back into antiquity, for them a pact could be made directly between man and God, without the intercession of a priest.

Receptive, therefore, to the idea that God could speak to them through a man such as Moses, the Jewish people seem to have allowed themselves not only to be led out of Egypt but also to accept, at Moses' instigation, an extraordinarily far-reaching code of conduct distinctively different from anything then known in the ancient world. While codes such as that of the Babylonian Hammurabi were essentially concerned with the protection of property, that of Moses was concerned minutely with how a man should conduct his life and behave towards his neighbour. There was a strong accent on humility and sympathy towards the poor, the widowed and the oppressed, considerations that were much lower in the priorities of other peoples. To emphasize God's universality, any attempt to limit him by some form of artistic representation was shunned. As a mark of his people's covenant with God (and, it seems, as a substitute for human sacrifice, Exodus 4: 24-6), every Jewish male child was circumcised. Typical of the way Mosaic Law permeated everyday life was the prohibition of eating certain meats. And all this was asked of and accepted by the Jewish people without any king or army of bully-boys to impose it. Military considerations seem eventually to have obliged the early Jewish people to accept kings, the first being the disastrous Saul, but even then each one was known as 'Messiah', or 'Anointed One' of God, and regarded as totally answerable to God

A 'miracle' of Moses, the finding of water in the desert for the twelve tribes of Israel. Like other *nabi'im*, Moses seems to have been proficient in certain forms of natural 'magic', such as water-divining. From a fresco of the third century AD in the synagogue at Dura-Europos. (At this provincial synagogue the normal Jewish prohibitions against human representation appear to have been relaxed.)

Anointing of David as king of the Jews. Kingly anointing was regarded as a magical act which imparted 'the spirit of God' (1 Samuel 16: 13). Jesus in his turn would have been regarded as filled with God's spirit (Matthew 3: 16) after his baptism by John the Baptist.

and the Torah, or Law of Moses. When King David committed adultery with one of his officers' wives, then neatly arranged for that officer to die in the front line, it was not a priest but a man like Moses, the prophet Nathan, who fearlessly stepped forward, despite David's popularity, to tell him his misdeeds, doing so by precisely the same parabolic method that Jesus employed to such effect a thousand years later. While in any other nation Nathan would have been instantly liquidated for his temerity, David, in precise accord with Mosaic guidelines, had the humility to recognize that Nathan was right, and to repent.

Whatever the authenticity of the Moses and Nathan stories, it was characteristic of the spirit of the Jewish people that whenever monarch, priesthood or nation went astray, some ordinary man or woman would simply appear and announce what he or she believed to be God's view on the matter. In Hebrew such individuals were known as *nabi'im*, literally mouthpieces of God. In modern religious teaching they are referred to as 'prophets', but this is really a misnomer since foretelling the future was usually the least of their many attributes. Most importantly, a *nabi* was not a priest *per se*. The Jewish people had priests by this time, but they were regarded, and would continue to be regarded, as mere functionaries, supervisors of animal sacrifices, and ultimately of no religious importance. A *nabi* could be anyone, a courtier such as Isaiah, priests such as Jeremiah and Ezekiel, even a woman, such as Deborah, but quite often an uncouth countryman, such as Elijah the Tishbite, who in the ninth century, clad in a goat's hair shirt, came forward to condemn Israel's King Ahab and his flagrantly pagan Queen Jezebel. A *nabi* was supremely important because he represented the voice of God, but his inevitable problem was that of convincing others that he was what he claimed to be. The surest sign was the working of what appeared to be 'miracles'. Moses reputedly first attracted notice by turning his rod into a snake, a story which, fantastic as it may sound, may well be true. A cobra, if given a sharp blow on the back of the neck, will go cataleptically rigid like a rod, as Egyptian snake-charmers can still demonstrate. Moses seems simply to have reversed the process. And he followed this trick with some water-divining in the desert. The common feature of *nabi'im* was a commanding, probably hypnotic personality which enabled them, as in the cases of Elijah and Elisha, to practise 'natural magic', sometimes returning 'dead' people to life.

Nabi'im, because they tended towards an ascetic, 'back to nature' outlook, continually railed against the Jewish people for lapsing into the hedonism and materialism that Moses had led them away from in Egypt. They warned

Antiochus IV Epiphanes (reigned 175–63 BC), Seleucid King of Syria. Modelling himself on Alexander the Great, he tried to stamp out the Jewish religion by prohibiting Mosaic customs and erecting a statue of Zeus in the Jerusalem Temple. His actions provoked the Maccabean revolt.

Jerusalem, showing the area of the city (north of the Kidron Valley) inhabited at the time of David and Solomon. Solomon built the first Temple on the elevation where the Dome of the Rock now stands. On this same site, levelled and extended, Herod the Great constructed the magnificent Second Temple of the time of Jesus. According to tradition, it was here that the patriarch Abraham had offered to sacrifice his only son Isaac.

that to ignore their words could spell disaster. Back in the eleventh century King David, motivated, it appears, principally by religious rather than strategic considerations, had chosen Jerusalem as his capital, and here his son Solomon, relishing grandeur, built the first Temple for the offering of animal sacrifices. In the sixth century the Babylonians swept in, destroyed the Temple and most of Jerusalem with it. They then hauled off the brightest and most able-bodied of Jewish survivors to captivity in Babylon, by whose waters, in the words of the Psalm, the prisoners sat down and wept.

It has been suggested that it was at this period that most of what we now know as the Old Testament may have been written, and that Jewish plagiarists of the time cribbed some of their material, such as the Flood story, from the Babylonians' early archives, or perhaps adapted it for use as propaganda for their own monotheism. Whatever the truth of this, certainly the acme in Jewish literature, exemplified by Isaiah and others, was reached no later than this time.

The very privations endured by Jewish people urged them to retain their distinctiveness from other peoples, a distinctiveness they were prepared to cling to and defend, even with their own lives, against any adversity that the future might hold for them. And it held plenty.

As an aid to understanding the religious and political climate in which Jesus grew up, some brief background information is needed concerning the Jewish people's struggle for survival during the centuries immediately preceding his birth. In 539 AD the Babylonians were conquered by Cyrus the Persian and the Jews allowed to return to their land and restore their Temple. Within two centuries, however, the relatively benevolent Persian rule was overthrown by Alexander the Great's crushing defeat of Darius at the battle of Issus. The Jewish people soon found themselves at the centre of a power struggle between two conflicting dynasties of Alexander's successors, the Seleucids of Mesopotamia and the Ptolemies of Egypt. One result of this was the insidious influence of exposure to a Hellenistic way of life, which brought with it wider political and commercial contacts. By the second century even priests had been lured by the attractions of Greek athletics and began neglecting their Temple duties and building Greek-style gymnasia. But in 167 AD matters came to a head when the Seleucid King Antiochus IV Epiphanes, modelling himself on Alexander, tried to impose a universal Hellenistic religion by the abolition of the Sabbath rest day, the prohibition of circumcision, the erection of Zeus' statue in the Jerusalem Temple, and the sacrifice of pigs on the Temple altars. Antiochus dealt forcefully with dissidence, destroying Jewish scriptures and burning alive anyone caught living by the rules of the Torah. According to the First Book of Maccabees, 'Women who had had their children circumcised were put to death ... with their babies hung round their necks' (1 Maccabees 1: 60, 61). Yet in the face of such adversity the ordinary people showed themselves to be neither swayed nor intimidated. A brilliant contemporary publicist wrote what we now know as the Book of Daniel, promising, in the form of an allegory set in Babylon, that a stone would destroy a mighty statue and bring about the return of God's kingdom. It seems to have provided just the right inspiration for guerilla resistance. An aged priest called Mattathias killed a fellow-Jew about to make a sacrifice to Zeus. Mattathias' five sons then took up the struggle, the leadership of their group passing from Judas (called Maccabeus – The Hammer), to Jonathan, and then to Simon. It was Simon who, as early as three years after the outbreak of resistance, was able to lead an ecstatic, palm-waving crowd back into the Temple to cleanse it from its pagan defilement, and rededicate it to the one true God.

For a century, as the Hasmonean dynasty (named after Mattathias' great-great-grandfather Hasmon), Simon's family clung to the uncertain and strife-torn independence of their prime territory, Judaea, at the same time, in a wave of evangelism, annexing and converting to Judaism former pagan territories such as Galilee and Idumea.

Then in 63 BC the Romans arrived. The Roman general Pompey, having conquered Syria a year earlier, marched his army into Jerusalem, finding serious resistance only at the Temple. He discovered that the Sabbath was a particularly good day on which to fight Jews. Following the rules of their Torah, they would not defend their walls on that day, only their own persons, and then at the very last resort. Intrigued by this strange religion of theirs, Pompey was curious to find out what lay in their Temple's Holy of Holies, entry to which he knew was prohibited to anyone but the Jewish high priest. As soon as he had secured his victory, he strode inside to find out for himself. He found it was nothing but a small, empty room, without even a window. What sort of religion was this?

Twenty-three years later the Romans accorded to the Jews the pretence of self-government by appointing as puppet king the Idumean Herod the Great, who had wormed his way into the Hasmonean family, and was loathed by his people from the very first. Acutely conscious of his own unpopularity, Herod systematically liquidated all whom he considered potentially dangerous to him, including his own wife and two of his sons, and surrounded himself with a network of informers and secret police as clandestine and ruthless as the KGB. Those three sons who survived followed in their father's footsteps when Herod died in 4 BC, though one, Archelaus, to whom had fallen Judaea, Idumaea and Samaria, failed to shape up to Roman requirements, and was replaced by direct Roman governorship.

It was into this unstable and power-torn world that Jesus was born. If we feel the need for independent corroboration of its stress and violence, we need look no further than a report by Israeli pathologist Dr Nicu Haas on the skeletons of inhabitants of a Herodian cemetery found in 1968 at Giv'at ha-Mivtar in northern Jerusalem. Of thirty-five skeletons examined, Haas identified no fewer than nine as victims of some form of violent death. One, a four-year-old child, had died in agony from an arrow that had struck and partially penetrated the left side of his skull. Another, a youth of seventeen, had stripes on his leg bones that indicated he had been slowly roasted to death bound to a rack, a human barbecue. Yet another, a woman of nearly sixty, had received a lethal blow from a mace-like instrument, shattering the back of her skull, and the bones of her upper back. A young man of about twenty-seven years of age had been executed by crucifixion.

← 324mm →

Leg-bone from seventeen-year-old youth whose remains were found in the Giv'at ha-Mivtar cemetery. The dark cross stripes are fire marks which indicate that the youth was probably fastened to a rack on which he was burnt alive. According to pathologists his body was then left on the fire for some considerable time after death. (Reproduced from N. Haas 'Anthropological Observations on the Skeletal Remains from Giv'at ha-Mivtar', *Israel Exploration Journal* Vol. 20, 1970.)

Yet it would be entirely wrong to give the impression that Rome and the Herods brought to the Jewish people a regime of unmitigated oppression. Superficially these were times of unprecedented prosperity, not least in matters of religion. It was Roman policy to tolerate established local beliefs, and perhaps in a move to ensure some affection from posterity, in 20–19 BC Herod the Great set in motion plans to make the Jerusalem Temple the largest and most magnificent religious building in the world. The platform on which it stood, built with huge blocks of stone, stretched a quarter of a mile long by a fifth of a mile wide. Gleaming gold plates were set up in the

The Temple of Herod, from the reconstruction by M. and E.
Avi-Yonah. The magnificent edifice raised mixed feelings:
Jesus' disciples are reported to have viewed it with awe (Mark
13: 1), but there was hatred for its builder, the Idumaean
Herod, and for the priestly aristocracy who controlled its affairs.

inner courts. From its ramparts silver trumpets heralded each dawn. Twenty thousand functionaries were employed in its servicing, and a further sixteen thousand craftsmen and labourers were drilled as construction and refurbishing teams that would be kept occupied for three quarters of a century. The courts, most of which were closed to Gentiles, and the Inner Court, barred to all but healthy, male Jews, teemed with animals and birds on sale for sacrifices. This was the one place, reputedly on the very spot where Abraham had once stayed his hand in sacrificing his son Isaac, that animal sacrifices were still practised within the Jewish religion. Here a man was judged on the scale of his offering, and the money used and re-used in elaborate banking transactions that had been learned from the Babylonians.

But was it not the *nabi* Isaiah who had commented as long as eight centuries ago:

This people honours me only with lip-service while their hearts are far from me. The worship they offer me is worthless, the doctrines they teach are only human regulations.

(Isaiah 29: 13)

Essentially the Temple expressed, by its very opulence, the intense separatism which by now had turned the Jewish religion into a highly quarrelsome, multi-party organism. All too obvious were the fine houses of the Sadducean priestly aristocracy, controllers of the Temple's extensive financial dealings. Since 1969 Israeli archaeologist Nachman Avigad has been patiently unearthing what remains of these once very large, stone-built Graeco-Roman villas with beautiful mosaic floors and frescoed walls. While features such as ritual *mikveh* for ablutions leave little doubt as to the owners' priestly occupations, there are also indications of luxurious living in evidence, such as the remains of amphorae of the finest blown glass that once held expensive imported wine. Although in theory the men who lived in such style were servants of the Temple of God, in practice, with their Hellenistic tastes, they were as much collaborators with the pagan Romans as the hated Herod had been. Because of the prevailing view that the only atonement for a man's sins was repentance and sacrifice – and the Temple was the only place where sacrifices could be made – they ran a valuable monopoly. In religious terms they clung to the letter of Moses' Torah, not its spirit, and denied belief in the resurrection of the body.

Such men were clearly a long way removed from those who remained in tune with the old, traditional spirit of the Jewish people, for whom God was not to be found in fancy palaces. And the Jewish religion, perhaps more

Remains of large Herodian house, which probably belonged to one of the hated Sadducean aristocracy; it was uncovered during recent excavations in Jerusalem. In the centre is a non-figurative mosaic floor, in keeping with the Torah's prohibition on human or animal images (Exodus 20: 4). Just to the foreground is a ritual basin for religious ablutions.

Qumran, remains of the monastery of the sect responsible for the Dead Sea Scrolls, generally thought to have been the Essenes who shunned the corruption Jewish worship had suffered in Jerusalem.

vibrant now than at any other time in its history, was not short of individuals and groups offering paths back to a true kingdom of God. For some, such as the Essenes, the sect thought to have been responsible for the Dead Sea Scrolls, the path was found by shutting themselves away in closed communities, sometimes in the desert, sharing all they had with their fellow men, leading a life of simplicity, and working and praying for the day when the stain of paganism could be removed from their land. For others, most notably the famous and maligned Pharisees, experts in scriptural interpretation, the way was found by remaining close to the ordinary people, working alongside them as humble tailors, shoemakers and the like, educating children, founding regional synagogues, and developing their own oral tradition of Jewish wisdom that, despite every attempt to suppress it, would flourish into present-day Judaism. Unlike the Sadduccees, they believed that the body would physically rise from the grave at the end of time, and for this reason insisted that the dead should be buried, not cremated, and all the bones left intact. By no means the dry-as-dust hypocrites represented in the gospels, the Pharisees, upholders of the spirit of the Law, seem to have been vigorous and down to earth, 'with the multitude on their side', as remarked by Josephus. Although they did not appear actively to oppose the Roman regime, they made no bones about their lack of love for it, and had what might be termed a para-military wing, the so-called Zealots, who from the days of Herod the Great had been making regular attempts at insurrection. Jesus' Galilee was known as a particularly important stronghold for the Zealots, it having been from this region that in 4 BC Zealot Judas Galileus led an assault on the royal arsenal at Sepphoris, four miles from Nazareth, returning ten years later, at the time of Quirinius' census, to urge the people not to pay their taxes to Rome. Although Mark's gospel is typically evasive about such a sensitive political issue (he omits to translate the Aramaic word for Zealot), the overall gospel record makes clear that Jesus had among his disciples one 'Simon called the Zealot' (Luke 6: 15). And Judas Iscariot, whose surname probably means 'daggerman', may have been in similar mould.

Also particularly strong in Galilee, not as a numerical party but as lone individuals with a powerful local impact, were the so-called *hasidim*, or 'devout ones', whose importance, and significance in association with Jesus, has been reaffirmed by Dr Geza Vermes. Very much like the *nabi* of old, the *hasid* cultivated an affirmity with God and a way of life that could not have been further removed from the ways of the Sadducean priesthood in Jerusalem. He was almost invariably a countryman, a typical example being Honi the Circle Drawer, possibly a Galilean and undoubtedly a powerful worker of natural magic during the first century BC. Once, during a time of drought, Honi is said to have drawn a circle around himself and vowed not to move out of it until rain came. Apparently the Almighty obliged, though Honi was later ungratefully stoned to death when he refused a mob's request to lay a curse on an unpopular politician. Another *hasid*, just a generation after Jesus, but from Araba, ten miles to Nazareth's north, was Hanina ben Dosa, particularly reputed as a healer, and again a figure very much in the *nabi* mould.

Linking all these separatist groups and individuals was a common urge to unify the Jewish people under God. But what was needed, as in the early days when their country was under dire threat from the Philistines, was another giant-killer, another David, as 'Messiah' or anointed one of God. Inevitably the different factions had their own ideas of what sort of man this Messiah should be. Not unexpectedly, to the Zealots he was predominantly a military figure, one who would drive out the Romans and set up an essentially temporal new kingdom of Israel, albeit under God. Others saw him as more spiritually oriented, a kind of super-*nabi*, the one of whom Moses himself had spoken when he wrote:

God will raise up for you a prophet like myself, from among yourselves, from your own brothers; to him you must listen ... I will put my words into his mouth and he shall tell them all I shall command him. (Deuteronomy 18: 15, 18)

No matter what sort of Messiah they believed in, however, no Jew expected him to be anything other than a human being. It was against this background, this seething cauldron of frustration against a world that was not as it should be, that Jesus grew up in Galilee. Nothing is known of any early influences that might have triggered in him a belief that God had some special purpose for him. In any case there was one prerequisite for any 'Messiah' – that his coming would be preceded by a return of the *nabi* Elijah. According to one view, the re-born Elijah would actually recognize and anoint the Messiah-to-be before that individual was himself aware of his identity. So where was an Elijah figure to be found in the early years of the first century AD? As if right on cue, on the shores of the Jordan appeared an extraordinary wild man dressed in camel-skins, the man the gospels call John the Baptist.

FLOUTER OF CONVENTION

WE can be reasonably certain that John the Baptist did once exist. Throughout early Christian literature he is referred to as a man of whom everyone has heard, and the New Testament book of Acts discloses that John's disciples carried his teachings as far afield as Alexandria and Ephesus (Acts 18: 25; 19: 2). Although the gospel authors are concerned predominantly with Jesus, and even suggest that a little rivalry existed between the disciples of John and those of Jesus, they acknowledge that great crowds had flocked to John from 'Jerusalem and all Judaea and the whole Jordan district' (Matthew 3: 5). One reason for John's attraction seems to have been that his baptisms offered an alternative to the Temple's monopoly on the cleansing of sins. If John had stirred up such a following we would expect him to have attracted attention from outside Christian literature, and sure enough Josephus mentions him in a passage that it is generally agreed was not a copyist's interpolation:

He was a good man, and exhorted the Jews to lead righteous lives, practise justice towards one another and piety towards God, and so to join in baptism. In his view this was a necessary preliminary if baptism was to be acceptable to God. They must not use it to gain pardon for whatever sins they committed, but as a consecration of the body, implying that the soul was thoroughly purified beforehand by right behaviour.

It is from Josephus that we learn that the young woman responsible for John's execution was named Salome.

As Dr Martin Pulbrook of Maynooth, Ireland, and others have argued, the full extent of John the Baptist's influence on Jesus has probably been played down in the gospels, particularly by the synoptic authors. Nevertheless, even if everything else related in the gospels about Jesus' early life is unreliable, the first event on which all sources are in agreement, the Mark and John gospels effectively beginning with it, is Jesus' baptism by John.

Jesus' baptism by John the Baptist, from a fifth-century mosaic in Santa Maria in Cosmedin, Ravenna. Note Jesus' nudity and the 'spirit of God' descending in the form of a bird.

One reason for believing that this actually happened lies in the fact that there was no advantage to be gained by the gospel writers from inventing it. Rather the reverse, as it implied that Jesus must have had sins that needed washing away. A hint of early Christian sensitivity on this matter is to be found in the Matthew gospel, which represents John the Baptist as saying to Jesus: 'It is I who need baptism from you', and Jesus replying, 'Leave it like this for the time being . . .' (Matthew 3: 15).

If John's baptism of Jesus actually occurred, what sort of event was it? The John gospel remarks that one of the settings in which the Baptist conducted his work was 'Aenon, near Salim, where there was plenty of water' (John 3: 23), and according to American archaeologist Professor W. F. Albright, this particular spot can almost certainly be identified to this day:

> ... Salim cannot be separated from the well known ancient town of that name, south-east of Nablus, nor can it be quite accidental that there is an 'Ainun in the immediate vicinity. The nearby sources of the Wadi Far'ah are extremely well provided with water.

In fact, the gospels are fairly explicit that Jesus' baptism was not necessarily at this location but somewhere else along the Jordan. An obvious deduction to be drawn, however, is that a baptism by John required an open-air location and a plentiful supply of fresh water, the intention, clearly, being total immersion. It also appears to have required the personal officiation of John or one of his disciples, and to have been, for each recipient, a unique event, there being no accounts of anyone returning for a second baptism.

In each of these respects the John baptism was distinctively different from the routine, self-administered ritual ablutions long commonplace for religious purification among Jews of all denominations. As indicated by the Josephus reference, it was a form of consecration or initiation by which, after repentance, an individual could feel purified from his past sins in preparation for a better life thereafter. According to the Matthew gospel, John proclaimed his baptism as preparation for the coming of the Kingdom of God (Matthew 3: 2).

We know enough of Jesus' baptism, his highly important first appearance on the stage of history, to be able to envisage something of the scene, with the hairy John in his camel-skins, and Jesus himself most likely naked for according to early churchman Hippolytus, and references to 'complete stripping' by Paul (1 Colossians 2: 11), that is how the earliest Christian baptisms seem to have been conducted. Since no source on John specifically describes witnesses at his baptisms, it may be that he somehow managed to impart a degree of privacy to each, thereby adding to the ceremony's element of mystery.

The very popularity of John's baptisms suggests that they had a powerful impact on those who received them and, we may assume, on no-one more so than on Jesus. We are told that as he surfaced he seemed to receive a vision in the form of a dove, accompanied by a heavenly voice announcing: 'You are my son ...' (Mark 1: 11). The sceptic might dismiss this as an obvious piece of Christian deification of Jesus, but it cannot be tossed aside so lightly. In orthodox Jewish tradition, the *hasid* Hanina ben Dosa was specifically associated with the hearing of a heavenly voice addressing him with the words: 'my son Hanina'. In the Jewish royal ritual a perfectly human King of the Jews became 'son of God' at the time of his anointing as Messiah. An especially intriguing feature of Jesus' baptism, to be found in all canonical gospels (and such non-canonical ones as the gospel of the Ebionites), is the association of a bird with his reported vision. As has been pointed out by Dr Morton Smith, the vision of a bird also occurs in early mystery religion initiations, as in one Greek magical papyrus description in which an initiate, after lying naked in a sheet and repeating a prescribed chant, is told to expect to see 'a sea-hawk flying down' as a sign that union with the deity had been achieved. Such initiations were commonly followed by a period of self-enforced privation, reminiscent of Jesus' 'forty days in the wilderness'.

It would not be unreasonable to interpret Jesus' baptism experience as having been a life-changing one. The John gospel even seems to suggest that Jesus initially became one of the Baptist's disciples, spreading his work into other areas (John 3: 22–24), and becoming even more successful at it (John 4: 1), although we are somewhat contradictorily told 'in fact it was his [Jesus'] disciples who baptised, not Jesus himself' (John 4: 2). Dr Morton Smith has suggested that this might be an inaccurate translation of an Aramaic statement that it was only his disciples whom Jesus himself baptized. Whatever Jesus' role in relation to John's baptisms, circumstances were to be dramatically changed by John's arrest. In the manner typical of a traditional *nabi*, it seems that John voiced God's disapproval of Herod the Great's son Herod Antipas, tetrarch of the Galilee and Peraea regions, who took as his second wife Herodias, the ex-wife of one of his brothers. Josephus, it is true, offers a different, though not necessarily incompatible reason for his arrest:

... Eloquence that had so great an effect on mankind might lead to some form of sedition, for it looked as though they would be guided by John in everything that they did. Herod decided therefore that it would be much better to strike first and be rid of him before his work led to an uprising.

Whatever the exact reason, Herod, unlike King David, was not the sort of man to accept criticism. He always had the Romans to call to his aid. Accordingly, even if Herod required a little encouragement from Herodias and Salome, John lost his head.

Given the profundity of Jesus' encounter with John, there can be little doubt of the impact this news would have had upon him. Although the Mark gospel details the circumstances of John's execution, as usual it steers clear of politics, the most we hear of Jesus' attitude to Antipas is two words from elsewhere in the gospels: 'that fox ...' (Luke 13: 32). What Mark does describe, in the very next breath, is a large crowd 'like sheep without a shepherd' who, with scant thought for provisions, immediately journeyed to a 'lonely place' to seek out Jesus. There were five thousand of them, and, as has been pointed out by Dr John Robinson, they were all men (Mark 6: 44). Exactly what happened on this occasion has been somewhat obscured in the gospels by the 'miracle' – the feeding of the five thousand – which they tell us took place. Whatever the background truth of this story, its origins are undoubtedly early: Mark had evidently drawn on two even earlier accounts of the event, one referring to five thousand people, the other to four thousand. According to Luke, John the Baptist taught that 'If anyone has two tunics he must share with the man who has none' (Luke 3: 11), and the 'miracle' might, therefore, be explained by Jesus simply having persuaded those who had brought food to the 'lonely place' to share with those who had not.

It seems clear that the popular following which John the Baptist had stirred up, the following so feared by Herod Antipas, had turned itself to Jesus, as John's star pupil, for its leadership. Jesus appears to have responded by taking up John's message, proclaiming the need for repentance, and the closeness of the kingdom of God (Mark 1: 15). But while he evidently impressed his audience on this occasion, hence the story of a miracle, he also seems to have displayed that same reluctance to become involved in politics that had caused charismatic Honi, the Circle Drawer, to be stoned a century before. According to the John gospel, immediately after the left-over food had been gathered up in baskets, 'Jesus could see they were about to come and take him by force and make him king' (John 6: 15). His response was to make a swift diplomatic exit to the hills.

In this lies one of the most explicit indications of Jesus' purpose. Had he been a mere guerilla leader, as some contend, he would have seized upon the wave of popular support, and there and then drawn up plans for a rebellion. But whatever John's baptism had instilled in him, it was not of this order. Rather there had been born or brought to the fore in him an intense affinity with God, an utter confidence that he was a child of God, and consequently anything and everything was possible. Even the Bultmann school of thought has recognized that those of Jesus' utterances that have been left in Aramaic have the greatest claim to authenticity, and of these undoubtedly one of the most striking is his habit of addressing God as 'Abba', meaning father. It must be recognized that, for most Jews, the very name of God carried such mystique that it could neither be uttered, nor set in writing. The earliest manuscript copies of the books of the Old Testament feature God's name in the form of the 'Tetragrammaton', four Hebrew letters, the equivalents of YHWH, or Yahweh with the vowels omitted, and usually written in a more archaic form than the rest of the text. When he came to these letters the reader automatically substituted *Adonai*, Hebrew for Lord. Yet for Jesus to address God so directly as 'Father' does not necessarily mean he claimed to be his divine son in the Christian sense. Rather, it was a form of address often used by the Jewish holy man, the *nabi*, the *hasid* or indeed anyone who felt he could enter into a direct dialogue with God. 'Abba' as a way of addressing God was certainly used by the grandson of Honi the Circle Drawer.

So Jesus, it seems, lived in a vivid and immediate kingdom of God within his own mind, the nearness of which, and the means of reaching it, he fervently wished to share with others. The Mark gospel tells us that when Jesus had been sought out by the five thousand in the 'lonely place', he 'set himself to teach them at some length' (Mark 6: 34), and while his exact message on that occasion has gone unrecorded, it may readily be deduced from such texts as the Matthew 'Sermon on the Mount':

Do not store up treasures for yourself on earth, where moths and woodworm destroy them and thieves can break in and steal ... You cannot be the slave both of God and money. That is why I am telling you not to worry about your life and what you are to eat, nor about your body and how you are to clothe it. Surely life means more than food and the body more than clothing? Look at the birds in the sky. They do not sow or reap or gather into barns; yet your heavenly Father feeds them. Are you not worth much more than they are? Can any of you, for all his worrying, add one single cubit to his span of life? And why worry about clothing? Think of the flowers in the fields; they never have to work or spin; yet I assure you that not even Solomon in all his regalia was robed like one of these. (Matthew 6: 19-29)

The message is an extraordinarily striking and compelling one. It has

Right A typical 'wilderness' scene. After John the Baptist's death, Jesus was sought out by a reputed five thousand male Jews at a remote place such as this.

Below 'They collected twelve basketfuls of scraps of bread and pieces of fish' (Mark 6: 43). Remarkably modern in appearance, this Jewish basket, from within a century of the time of Jesus, was found in the remote caves used by rebels during the Bar-Kokhba revolt.

90

inspired all sorts of men and women – St Francis of Assisi, William Blake, Tolstoy, Mother Teresa of Calcutta, even a non-Christian such as Mahatma Gandhi. In conventional Christianity sufficient attention is rarely paid to it, but ultimately it may be distilled into a simple attitude of mind: self-abnegation, shedding the earthly bonds of property, clothes, family ties and the like, and dwelling in a heaven of the mind. Almost everything Jesus said and did can be related to this utterly simple and consistent way of thought. He also imparted a sense of urgency: men must follow this teaching before it was too late, before God took matters into his own hands. This attitude of mind lay behind his reputedly telling a bereaved man: 'leave the dead to bury their dead' (Matthew 8: 22). It lay behind his telling a rich young man who wanted to be perfect, 'Go and sell everything you own and give the money to the poor' (Matthew 19: 21). It lay behind his counselling extreme pacifism: 'offer the wicked man no resistance. On the contrary, if anyone hits you on the right cheek, offer him the other also' (Matthew 5: 39–40).

Too often Christian writers imply that Jesus introduced such doctrines as if they were utterly new, in a world that had heard nothing like them before. But this needs careful qualification. Jesus' saying 'If a man . . . would have your tunic, let him have your cloak as well' (Matthew 5: 41) is essentially little different from John the Baptist's: 'If anyone has two tunics he must share with the man who has none'. The end product of Jesus' essentially communist outlook is graphically conveyed in the book of Acts' description of how his followers lived in Jerusalem after his death: '. . . all lived together and owned everything in common; they sold their goods and possessions and shared out the proceeds among themselves according to what each one needed' (Acts 2: 45). And this is no different from what we are told of the Essenes by Josephus: 'each man's possessions go into the pool', and as with brothers their entire property belongs to them all. Similarly, just as Jesus sent his disciples on their missions 'with no haversack for the journey or spare tunic or footwear' (Matthew 10: 10), so we are told of the Essenes, '. . . when they travel they carry no baggage at all, but only weapons to keep off bandits . . . Neither garments nor shoes are changed till they are dropping to pieces or worn out with age'. Such parallels might seem to diminish Jesus' originality; certainly they reveal that many of his ideas were simply typical of the best of Jewish spiritual thought of his time. But it is also clear that time and again Jesus gave an existing idea a new twist, and not always in the same direction. John the Baptist asked for the man with two tunics to give away the one he did not need; Jesus asked him, if called upon, to give away both. The book of Leviticus ruled: 'You must love your neighbour as yourself' (Leviticus 19: 18); Jesus urged, 'Love your *enemies*, and pray for those who persecute you' (Matthew 5: 44). Such precepts, so far as can be ascertained, were utterly new, and exclusive to the gospel Jesus. They have no obvious counterparts in the teachings of either the Pharisees or the Essenes. Humane and inspired as the old Mosaic code is, they go far beyond it.

It is in this new emphasis that we see the truly original, unconventional Jesus, just as we see him in the form of teaching that he made more vivid and compelling than ever before, the parable.

Even the Bultmann school has been prepared to acknowledge that the gospel material that is most likely to be authentic to Jesus (though probably not without some fabrication and re-touching) is his parables, some thirty or forty of which are to be found in the synoptic gospels. This view is borne out by the fact that if he, as a flesh and blood historical figure, had not invented them, we should be obliged to look for someone equally remarkable who had. In fact, they have precisely the same individual quality that distinguishes his teachings. If they were facile forgeries, put into the mouth of a man who never existed, we would expect the rich man always to be the villain, the self-righteous man always to be the hero – but this is far from being the case: they always have an element of the unexpected in relation to normal morality.

This is the historical Jesus at his most strange, and also his most convincing. In their Mosaic Law the Jews had already advanced millennia compared to their 'civilized' neighbours in expressing sympathy for the poor, the widowed and the oppressed. Jesus did not ask for this Law to be re-written; he clearly acknowledged that it still formed the proper basis for human conduct:

> Do not imagine that I have come to abolish the Law or the prophets . . . till heaven and earth disappear not one dot, not one little stroke, shall disappear from the Law . . . (Matthew 5: 17, 18)

But he seems to have believed there to be all sorts of circumstances in which love should transcend the Law to embrace individuals whose sinfulness had in Jewish eyes rendered them 'unclean', and thus unfit to worship God. In the parable of the prodigal son, conventional justice would seem to be squarely on the side of the son who had dutifully stayed at home to mind his half of his father's estate, while his prodigal brother squandered his share in riotous living. Yet to Jesus the virtuous one's objections to the welcome his brother received were of no account. It was the prodigal on whom attention should be lavished, like the lost sheep or the lost penny. Similarly, while in conventional Jewish society anyone who had indulged in immoral behaviour, such as a prostitute, or who had collaborated with the Romans, such as a tax-collector, would be considered an outcast, Jesus is represented as deliberately seeking such people out. In this he seems to have followed in the footsteps of John the Baptist who, as Jesus himself remarked, attracted his own following of tax-collectors and prostitutes (Matthew 21: 32). The same unconventional approach has also been noted by Dr Geza Vermes as typical of other Jewish *nabi* and hasidic holy men.

So frequently do the gospels remark on Jesus' association with undesirables, enjoying meals with them, speaking of himself as 'a glutton and a drunkard' (Luke 7: 34), even declining to join in fasts observed by John the Baptist's disciples – behaviour which could only be seen by God-fearing Jews as leading unavoidably to a loss of ritual cleanliness – that there can be little doubt that he did behave in precisely this way. The most extreme example of such behaviour to be found in the canonical gospels is his acceptance of particularly intimate favours from 'a woman ... who had a bad name in the town' (Luke 7: 37). This woman is described as wiping Jesus' feet with her hair, massaging his feet and/or his head with an expensive lotion, and lavishing kisses upon him. The incident appears to have been such an emotive one for gospel writers and disciples alike that no two accounts are the same, Luke concentrating on the horror felt by Jesus' host at the fact that he allowed himself to be made impure by such a woman, the Matthew, Mark and John writers noting instead the disciples' consternation at the waste of money:

> Why this waste of ointment? Ointment like this could have been sold for over three hundred denarii and the money given to the poor. (Mark 14: 5)

Although everyone else appears embarrassed and angry, Jesus accepts the favours with a quite shameless equanimity.

It must be recognized that in Jesus' day almost any association with a woman outside one's immediate family was frowned upon. The Babylonian Talmud has a story of the Galilean Rabbi Yose being scolded for merely asking a woman the way to Lydda: 'You stupid Galilean, have the Sages not commanded "Do not engage in a lengthy conversation with a woman!"' In first-century Jewish society women were second-class citizens, banned from the Inner Courts of the Temple, banned from any part of the Temple during their monthly periods, and, at any time, instantly divorceable by their husbands without any right of redress, merely by the writing of a notice to this

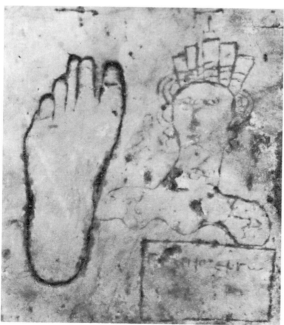

Above Jewish woman's hair, first century AD, from the excavations at Masada. Although Jewish women were regarded as second-class citizens in his time, Jesus flouted convention by entering into deep conversations with them, and included several among his followers.

Left A brothel sign, from a Graeco-Roman pavement in Ephesus. Jesus is said to have allowed himself to be fawned over by a well-known prostitute (Luke 7: 36–50), and is repeatedly described as associating with society's outcasts.

effect. Because the apostle Paul had never known the human Jesus, he reflected the attitudes of contemporary society towards women rather than Jesus' own ideas:

... women are to remain quiet at meetings since they have no permission to speak; they must keep in the background as the Law itself lays it down. If they have any questions to ask, they should ask their husbands at home: it does not seem right for a woman to raise her voice at meetings. (1 Corinthians 14: 35)

Yet Jesus is represented as entering into deep conversations with women, as in John 4: 27, 'The disciples returned and were surprised to find him speaking to a woman', and in Luke 10: 38-42, in which he becomes involved in such a lengthy discourse with Mary, sister of Martha of Bethany that even the practical Martha thinks he has gone too far. Although the gospels gloss over the fact, according to Luke Jesus appears to have had nearly as many women followers as men:

With him went the twelve, as well as certain women who had been cured of evil spirits and ailments: Mary surnamed the Magdalen, from whom seven demons had gone out, Joanna the wife of Herod's steward Chuza, Susanna and several others who provided for them out of their own resources. (Luke 8: 1-3)

Inevitably there has been a great deal of speculation as to why, in an age when Jewish priests and rabbis were very much expected to marry, Jesus should apparently have chosen not to do so. Inspired by certain mysterious references such as the 'disciple Jesus loved .. : leaning back on Jesus' breast' (John 13: 23-25), in the 1960s Anglican Bishop Hugh Montefiore put forward the idea that Jesus might have been a homosexual as 'an explanation we must not ignore'. Bishop Montefiore found few prepared to support the idea. Of altogether more popular appeal – judging by the success of *The Holy Blood and the Holy Grail* by Baigent, Leigh and Lincoln – has been the possibility that Jesus may secretly have married Mary Magdalen, the most often mentioned of the women followers. More fuel has been added by the discovery, among the Nag Hammadi hoard, of a 'gospel of Philip' which relates that:

... the companion of the [Saviour is] Mary Magdalen. [But Christ loved] her more than [all] the disciples, and asked to kiss her [often] on her [mouth]. The rest of [the disciples were offended] ... They said to him, 'Why do you love her more than all of us?' The Saviour answered and said to them, 'Why do I not love you as [I love] her.'

It should be emphasized, however, that the gospel of Philip, unlike its companion 'gospel of Thomas', has no special claim to an early date, and may be merely a fantasy of a type not at all uncommon among Christian apocryphal literature of the third and fourth centuries.

The real clues to why Jesus remained unmarried may perhaps lie in a cryptic remark in the Matthew gospel:

... there are eunuchs who make themselves that way for the sake of the kingdom of heaven (Matthew 19: 12)

and an equally significant passage in the Luke gospel:

The children of this world take wives and husbands, but those who are judged worthy of a place in the other world and in the resurrection from the dead do not marry because they can no longer die, for they are the same as the angels, and being children of the resurrection they are sons of God. (Luke 20: 34-37)

Jesus may well have been defining here a blueprint for human existence and for reaching the kingdom of God, and this would be totally consistent with his philosophy of self-abnegation. Although for most Jews the kingdom of God, long spoken of by the *nabi'im*, was conceived of as something between a politically independent state of Israel and a heavenly dream home for the righteous, for Jesus it seems to have been both of these – hence his talk of the 'coming' of the kingdom – and also something much more immediate, a freedom from all earthly ties. As Dr John Robinson beautifully expressed it in his controversial *Honest to God*, Jesus 'emptied himself utterly of himself', thus abandoning all self-consciousness, all shame, all self-seeking, in order that God and only God could shine through.

Repugnant though it might sound, if Jesus reappeared today his haunts would undoubtedly be the red light district of the big city, mixing with the pimps, prostitutes and con men, in line with his words: 'I did not come to call the virtuous, but sinners' (Mark 2: 17). A danger inherent in following such an unconventional philosophy is the extent to which it could be mis-understood, both then and today. On the strength of Jesus' association with sinners, and of his own remarkable secret gospel findings, Dr Morton Smith has interpreted Jesus as a hedonistic libertine. Smith imparts a heavy sexual innuendo to the nudity of the baptismal rite he believes Jesus to have practised, and suggests that, transported by his experiences of the kingdom of God, Jesus thought himself above the constraints of the Jewish Law, and able to do as he pleased. Secret nudity may perhaps have played a part in his baptisms. Independently of the 'secret gospel', this is attested by the can-onical gospels' reticence and contradictions concerning baptisms carried out by Jesus himself, by passages such as the gospel of Thomas's promise that Jesus would be revealed '... when you disrobe without being ashamed', and by a striking emphasis on the Adam and Eve story in the earliest Christian art. Another favourite and possibly significant early artistic theme was that of Jonah; having been swallowed by the whale, he was depicted 'reborn' naked in a beautiful garden, a clear symbol of the death and rebirth philosophy behind Christian baptism. Jesus may simply have wanted an innocent return to a Garden of Eden state and perhaps it was no coincidence that his favourite night meeting place was a garden (Luke 21: 37; John 18: 1, 2).

But however unconventional Jesus' behaviour may have been, he upheld the Jewish Law (Matthew 5: 17, 18). While telling the adulterous woman her sins were forgiven, he asked her not to repeat them (John 8: 11). He insisted on stricter, not more liberal divorce laws (Mark 10: 10), removing the male prerogative of dismissal of a wife. It was the underlying spirit of the Law that he wished to enforce rather than the letter of the Law. In conflict again with the hedonistic image, it was not only prostitutes and tax-collectors whom Jesus won over. Those who went on, after his death, to carry out his message, often at great danger to themselves, were ordinary, God-fearing people who, though they may sometimes have been shocked to observe him saying and doing things not expected of a holy man, followed him nonetheless. The strength of this following is in fact one of the most striking features of Jesus' recorded life. Repeatedly the gospels refer to the crowds which surrounded him wherever he went, crowds from whom, equally repeatedly he felt obliged to slip away when the pressure became too great. The Mark gospel comments on the predicament this presented for him:

Jesus could no longer go openly into any town, but had to stay outside in places where nobody lived. Even so, people from all around would come to him. (Mark 1: 45)

So great was the pull Jesus could exert, according to the gospels, that when he wanted helpers he had merely to say: 'Follow me', and hard-headed fishermen like Peter, James and John, a mercenary tax-collector like Matthew, and even a near-terrorist like Simon the Zealot, would abandon all else to do just that. Although a non-Christian, even Josephus, in the brief reference to Jesus discussed in chapter three, went so far as to tell us, 'He attracted many of the Jews and many of the Greeks'.

But no teaching alone, however unconventional or innovative, could have made such an impact. So what was it about Jesus that had such magnetic appeal?

MAN OF MIRACLES

... after sunset they brought to him all who were sick and those who were possessed by devils. The whole town came crowding round the door. (Mark 1: 32)

THERE is in fact no mystery as to why Jesus created such an impact. If there is one feature of his activities that repeatedly shines out from the gospels, it is his capacity to work what men have called 'miracles'. In this he was essentially following a tradition set by the *nabi* and the *hasid*, but with astonishing expertise. Although Moses and Elisha had been accredited with curing a leper or two (Numbers 12: 13; 2 Kings 5: 1–4), this feat was as nothing compared to the cases of paralysis, lameness, fever, catalepsy, haemorrhage, skin disease and mental disorder said to have been tackled by Jesus. Miracles were reportedly the first aspect of Jesus' ministry that Peter recalled after the resurrection:

Jesus the Nazarene was a man commended to you by God by the miracles and portents and signs that God worked through him when he was among you as you all know. (Acts 2: 22)

Jesus' reputation in this field was clearly what Josephus had in mind when he spoke of him as 'a wise man' who performed 'astonishing feats', or 'paradoxical deeds'. Josephus' choice of the word *paradoxon* is one commonly found to denote 'miracle' in Hellenistic Judaism. In the earliest Christian art, among the most common representations of Jesus are ones showing him with a magician's wand, usually raising Lazarus. As represented in the gospels, when Jesus was asked by the imprisoned John the Baptist whether he was 'the one who is to come (i.e. the super-*nabi* prophesied by Moses, Deuteronomy 18: 15–18), his reply to John's messengers was, 'Go back and tell John what you have seen and heard: the blind see again, the lame walk, lepers are cleansed, and the deaf hear, the dead are raised to life . . .' (Luke 7: 20–2).

That Jesus performed deeds that men called 'miracles' is therefore one of the best attested items of information about him. Yet paradoxically, it has

99

been one of the least explored because, as Matthew Arnold succinctly expressed it, 'miracles do not happen'. Under the influence of Kant and Hegel, the German rationalist theologians studiously resisted treating the gospel miracle stories seriously, and among many this resistance continues to this day. Nonetheless, in some areas of modern scholarship there has been a change of emphasis. Some people favour the idea that one of the earliest lost gospels may have been one specifically devoted to accounts of Jesus' miracles. Canon Anthony Harvey of Westminster Abbey, a leading Anglican scholar, has pointed out what he sees as the matter-of-fact quality of the miracle stories:

> In general one can say that the miracle stories in the gospels are unlike anything else in ancient literature ... They do not exaggerate the miracle or add sensational details, like the authors of early Christian hagiography [lives of the saints]; but nor do they show the kind of detachment, amounting at times to scepticism, which is found in Herodotus or Lucian ... To a degree that is rare in the writings of antiquity, we can say, to use a modern phrase, that they tell the story straight ...

If we allow ourselves at least temporarily to suspend incredulity towards miracles *per se*, we find that some of the stories have within them material which we simply cannot dismiss out of hand. For instance, in a manner rare among gospel stories, the writer of John, in one of his important narrative sections, sets the healing of the so-called paralytic in a historically identifiable building:

> Now at the Sheep Pool in Jerusalem there is a building, called Bethzatha in Hebrew, consisting of five porticoes; and under these were crowds of sick people – blind, lame, paralysed – waiting for the water to move; for at intervals ... the water was disturbed, and the first person to enter the water after this disturbance was cured of any ailment he suffered from ... (John 5: 1-4)

As a result of exhaustive research by Professor Joachim Jeremias, there can be no doubt that in Jesus' time Jerusalem had a building of this kind. Despite the depredations the city suffered, the building seems still to have existed in the fourth century. As reported by Western Europe's earliest Christian pilgrim to the Holy Land, the so-called Bordeaux pilgrim:

> Further in the city are twin pools having five porticoes, which are called Bethsaida. There those who have been sick for many years are cured. The pools contain water which is red when it is disturbed.

In subsequent centuries the five porticoes effectively disappeared as the building was converted into a church. This church in its turn suffered all

Remains of Herodian building (at lowest
level) thought to have been the five-porticoed
edifice housing the so-called Sheep Pool at
which Jesus is reported to have healed the
paralytic (John 5: 1–9).

sorts of vicissitudes as Jerusalem successively changed hands between Christians and Moslems. But the site has continued to be marked by a church, and it is here, at the church of St Anne, that excavations this century have revealed the remains of two huge rock-cut cisterns which undoubtedly once comprised the original Sheep Pool described by John, some of the masonry being of the time of Herod the Great.

If we can actually identify a building where Jesus once reputedly worked a miracle, can we perhaps trust the miracle itself a little more? We are told that the paralysed man had had his condition for thirty-eight years, and that Jesus cured him with the simple command: 'Get up, pick up your sleeping-mat and walk' (John 5: 8). This is obviously scant information on which to base any belief in the story, but as is well known medically, some paralyses are 'hysterical' in origin, that is they have a mental rather than physical cause, usually as a result of some severe emotional stress. Symptoms of this kind are particularly common during wartime, and as we have learned from Dr Nicu Haas's graphic account of the skeletal remains at the Giv'at ha-Mivtar cemetery, there would have been no shortage of causative stresses in Jesus' time. Besides paralysis, hysteria can induce disfiguring skin conditions, blindness, apparent inability to hear or speak, and all manner of symptoms of mental illness. An important feature of hysterical disorders is that the patient has no conscious awareness of feigning such symptoms. To him or her they are all too real, and they may last for many years. But unlike a physical condition with a non-reversible cause, hysterical disorders can be cured by the original, debilitating emotional problem being reached and released, today usually via drugs, psychotherapy or hypnosis. When effected the 'cure' can be dramatically sudden, and undoubtedly many so-called 'faith-healings' may be explained by this process, the trigger essentially being a form of hypnosis induced by the so-called 'faith-healer'.

It has to be acknowledged that even to this day no-one really knows what hypnosis is, even if hypnotists themselves will sometimes claim to know. In essence it appears to be a belief system between two individuals, one, the subject, abandoning himself, in terms of his waking consciousness, to another, the hypnotist, who by access to the patient's unconscious mind may be able to release elements that the consciousness has held back. So-called 'hysterical' individuals seem to make particularly good hypnotic subjects, and one consistent feature of such cases is that the effects of hypnosis tend to correspond to the degree of awe and authority the hypnotist is able to command. Understandably, the scientific world has been cautious in its approach to hypnosis because the process continues to hold so many mysteries and uncertainties. But few would now deny that it can produce some spectacular 'cures'.

The British hypnotist Peter Casson, well known for both stage and medical work, has on his files the case of a woman who, for fifteen years after a major car accident, was quite unable to close her hand or to grip with it. Although several operations failed to improve her condition, after only one hypnosis session with Peter Casson she found that she could once again close her hand and use it normally. Effectively, her 'cure' was achieved by commands little different from those which Jesus is said to have used in curing the paralytic by Jerusalem's Sheep Pool.

An even better attestation of the medical powers of hypnosis is a British doctor's quite dramatic use of it as a last resort in the cure of a particularly disfiguring skin condition, recorded, with accompanying photographs, in the *British Medical Journal* of 23 August 1952. Two years earlier a sixteen-year-old boy had been admitted to East Grinstead's Royal Victoria Hospital suffering from ichthyosis which, since birth, had covered his body with a black, horny, reptilian layer as uncomfortable and evil-smelling as it was disfiguring. Two attempts at plastic surgery were made, in both cases the freshly grafted skin soon taking on the reptilian appearance of the skin it replaced. Even Sir Archibald McIndoe, the most eminent plastic surgeon of the day, pronounced further attempts at conventional treatment useless. By chance, however, the boy's plight came to the notice of a young physician with an interest in hypnosis, Dr A.A. Mason, today a psychoanalyst in Beverly Hills, California, Dr Mason asked if he might at least try hypnosis to cure him, and on 10 February 1951, having induced a hypnotic state, he suggested to the youth that his left arm's reptilian layer would disappear. There ensued an extraordinary transformation. Within five days the horny covering on this arm simply fell away, and within a further few days the skin was soft, pink and normal for the first time in the boy's life. During the next few weeks hypnotic suggestion was given for the clearance of the reptilian layer on the right arm and then for specific remaining areas of his body, each time with between 50 per cent and 95 per cent success. The cure was slower than it might have been in the case of, say a hysterical blindness or paralysis, almost certainly because of the very nature of the disease. Indeed it is little short of incredible that the transformation should have happened at all. Because of the rarity of ichthyosis, Dr Mason failed to realize at the time that he was dealing not with some form of hysterical or similar condition but with a deep-seated congenital, structural illness. Had he been better in-formed he would most likely not have attempted hypnosis – to medical

Below left and right Hypnotic cure of a deeply disfiguring skin disorder. Before hypnosis the legs of Dr Mason's sixteen-year-old patient were covered with a repulsive reptilian layer (left). After verbal suggestion the horny layer fell away and was replaced by normal skin (right).

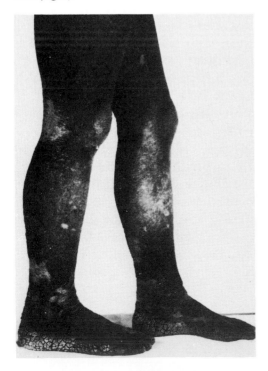

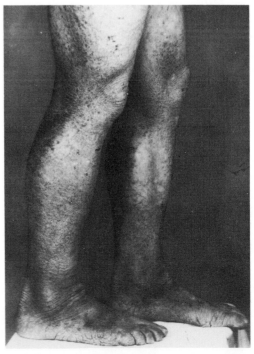

Above Knowledge of hypnosis in antiquity is suggested by this Egyptian Magical Papyrus in the British Museum. According to some interpretations, the text describes trance induction using a light source.

Jesus healing a so-called 'leper' (Mark 1: 40–42). In the ancient world 'leprosy' could denote a variety of disfiguring skin conditions. Details from a fifth-century ivory from Palermo, Sicily, now in the Victoria and Albert Museum, London.

history's loss. Dr. F. Ray Bettley, then president of the dermatological section of the Royal College of Medicine, considered the case to be little less inexplicable than if a club foot had been corrected, and that it indicated the need for a fundamental revision of existing concepts of the mind-body relationship. As far-reaching as any cure claimed of Jesus, it is the most striking possible attestation of what mere words, given the hypnotic state, can do.

Was there, however, a knowledge of hypnosis in ancient times on which Jesus might have drawn? Professor Lionel Haward of the University of Surrey psychology department has pointed out that some Egyptian papyri, such as the Demotic Magical Papyrus preserved in the British Museum, appear to describe hypnotic inductions and trance states, and these almost certainly formed part of the initiations into the mystery religions. There are classical frescoes that seem to depict individuals in trance states. That whatever Jesus was using for his miracles was not an exclusive appurtenance of divinity, but was well within the powers of ordinary men, is quite evident from the gospels themselves, which describe him sending out his disciples to do the same healing work that he undertook himself:

> He summoned his twelve disciples, and gave them authority over unclean spirits with power to cast them out, and to cure all kinds of diseases and sickness. (Matthew 10: 1)

Perhaps, then, hypnosis provides the key to understanding, and believing, at least some of Jesus' reputed miracles. If we look yet more closely at some of those attributed to him, we find good reason for trusting the gospel description of each sufferer's symptoms and for believing that Jesus used a type of hypnosis in effecting a cure. This applies particularly in exorcisms or cures from 'possession'.

In the early 1920, ironically at the University of Tübingen, scene of so many theological attacks on the gospels' credibility, Professor of Psychology T.K. Oesterreich produced a special study of the cases of possession encountered by Jesus, for publication in the journal *Deutsche Psychologie*. Subsequently he developed his research into a 400-page book *Possession, Demoniacal and Other*. Professor Oesterreich found the concise and clinical accounts of exorcisms in the Mark gospel particularly impressive. There was the so-called Gerasene demoniac:

> ... no sooner had he (Jesus) left the boat than a man with an unclean spirit came out of the tombs towards him. The man lived in the tombs, and no-one could secure him any more, even with a chain; because he had often been secured with fetters and chains but had snapped the chains and broken the fetters and no-one had the

strength to control him. All night and all day, among the tombs and in the mountains, he would howl and gash himself with stones . . . (Mark 5: 1–10).

There was the man suffering from convulsions:

In their synagogue . . . there was a man possessed by an unclean spirit and it shouted 'What do you want with us, Jesus of Nazareth? Have you come to destroy us?' . . . But Jesus said sharply 'Be quiet! Come out of him!' And the unclean spirit threw the man into convulsions and with a loud cry went out of him. (Mark 1: 23–27).

There was the youth who foamed at the mouth:

A man answered him from the crowd 'Master, I have brought my son to you; there is a spirit of dumbness in him, and when it takes hold of him it throws him to the ground, and he foams at the mouth and grinds his teeth and goes rigid. And I asked your disciples to cast it out and they were unable to . . . They brought the boy to him and as soon as the spirit saw Jesus it threw the boy into convulsions, and he fell to the ground and lay writhing there, foaming at the mouth. Jesus asked the father: 'How long has this been happening to him?' 'From childhood', he replied, 'and it has often thrown him into the fire and into the water, in order to destroy him . . .' (Mark 9: 17-27).

As commented by Professor Oesterreich:

. . . the succinct accounts of Jesus' relation to these events, his success and failure together with that of his disciples, as well as the particulars of his cures, coincide so exactly with what we know of these states from the point of view of present-day psychology that it is impossible to avoid the impression that we are dealing with a tradition which is veracious.

Of course, neither Professor Oesterreich nor any other realistic individual would explain a state of possession as the work of real demons or unclean spirits. But, irrespective of logic, the sufferer has come to believe himself so afflicted, again generally as a result of some emotional stress. However extreme the book and film of William Blatty's *The Exorcist* may appear, it is representative of a phenomenon that may be found reported century after century, throughout all sorts of cultures, both before and after the time of Jesus. In 1973, in West Yorkshire, a young father, believing himself to be possessed by devils, returned home from the meeting of a local religious group and murdered his wife and the family dog. A priest currently working in London, the Reverend Christopher Neil-Smith, has claimed to conduct up to five hundred exorcisms in the course of a single year. A less extreme form of possession is the condition known today as 'multiple personality', of which recent famous cases have been those of Virginia housewife Chris Sizemore (the original 'Eve' of *The Three Faces of Eve*), who in the course of as many years was possessed by some twenty different personalities, and Ohio rapist Billy Milligan, who in 1979 committed a series of robberies and rapes while apparently possessed by some nine alternating characters, ranging from 'Ragan', a hit-man, to a three-year-old girl, 'Christine', whose main preoccupation was painting butterflies. Among many parallels between these cases and those reputedly cured by Jesus, is a tendency for one of the personalities to speak for the rest by using the term 'us'. It occurs in the case of the Gerasene demoniac, who, asked his name by Jesus, tells him: 'My name is legion . . . for there are many of us' (Mark 5: 10). It occurs in the case of the 'Jane' personality of Chris Sizemore and the 'Vicky' personality of another such case written up by Flora Rheta Schreiber in *Sybil*, '. . . the rest of us know about Sybil, she knows nothing about any of us . . .'. But why, even if we can accept that Jesus came across genuine cases of possession, should we believe that he dealt with them by hypnosis? The answer is a circuitous one. The various methods known to have been used by exorcists and psychiatrists alike to deal with such cases may effectively be distilled into a single one. In each case an authority or power – a 'belief system' – is imposed on the one in which the possessed sufferer is trapped, essentially hypnosis. Jesus is consistently described in the gospels as using a sharp, authoritative manner in dealing with cases of possession and similar conditions: 'Be quiet! Come out of him!' (Mark 1: 26), '*Ephphatha!*' ('Be opened!') (Mark 7: 34), '*Talitha kum!*' ('Little girl, I tell you to get up!') (Mark 5: 41), leaving little doubt that Jesus' methods were similar. In the last two examples the gospels even provide us with his precise Aramaic words. We do not have to look far to discover who might have taught him his techniques. One of the most characteristic features of the charismatic *hasidim*, such as Honi the Circle Drawer and Hanina ben Dosa, is their practise of exorcism, arguably developing their own particular style and school of hypnosis. Hanina, like Jesus, was accredited with having cured a sick child from a distance, and was regarded as having made himself so proficient at exorcisms that he had mastered even Agrath, the daughter of Mahlath, queen of the demons. In his turn, Jesus passed on his exorcist powers to his disciples just as he gave them the ability to perform other cures. As we learn from Acts, they carried on his work after his death:

> There were . . . unclean spirits that came shrieking out of many who were possessed, and several paralytics and cripples were cured. (Acts 8: 7)

As Dr Geza Vermes has commented, it was typical of Jewish popular religion, in Galilee particularly, to attribute disorders to 'unclean spirits'.

Jesus was not, therefore, in any way unique in possessing the power to exorcise. That such practices were relatively common, and not always successful, is well illustrated by an Acts account of a bungled attempt at exorcism by the sons of the Jewish chief priest Sceva:

... the man with the evil spirit hurled himself at them and handled them so violently that they fled from the house naked and badly mauled. (Acts 19: 13-16).

But in the sheer scale of his reported successes Jesus was without equal, which tells us a great deal about the power of personality he was able to exert. Two special attributes appear to have enhanced this. One was his personal conviction that God was speaking and working through him in a manner unparalleled since the days of Moses (the Luke author represents him as speaking of 'the finger of God' as responsible for the success of his exorcisms, Luke 11:20). The other was an equally strong belief that at some unpredictable moment the dread 'Last Times' (already spoken of by earlier prophets) would begin, bringing eternal life for those who followed his words, and eternal damnation for those who did not. He would have been a difficult man to ignore.

An important indication of the basic honesty of the gospel writers' reporting of the healings and exorcisms is their admission, though it was sometimes reluctant, that Jesus' disciples occasionally failed in their attempts at this work (e.g. Mark 9: 19), and that even Jesus himself could fail. In his case, it is intriguing to note where the failure occurred:

... he went to his home town ... and ... they said 'Where did this man get all this? ... This is the carpenter, surely, the son of Mary, the brother of James and Joset ... And they would not accept him ... and he could work no miracle there ... (Mark 6: 1-6)

The gospel writers all appear to have been deeply embarrassed by this particular episode. To soften the blow a little Mark felt obliged to add 'though he cured a few people by laying his hands on them'. Matthew altered the last phrase to 'he did not work many miracles there' (Matthew 13: 58). Luke took the none too creditable step of replacing the whole account with one largely made up from other sources (Luke 4: 16-30), apparently trying to explain away the incident without actually specifying what it was.

The significance of this episode is that Jesus failed precisely where *as a hypnotist* we would most expect him to fail, among those who knew him best, those who had seen him grow up as an ordinary child. Largely responsible for any hypnotist's success are the awe and mystery with which he surrounds himself, and these essential factors would have been entirely lacking in Jesus'

Three miracles? *Above* Jesus healing a blind man (Mark 8: 22–6). *Below* During a wedding feast at Cana Jesus changes water into 'wine' (John 2: 1–10). Details from fifth-century ivory from Palermo, Sicily, now in the Victoria and Albert Museum, London.

Opposite Jesus raises Lazarus from 'death' (John 11: 1–44). According to Dr Morton Smith Lazarus was probably in a death-like trance, during which he experienced a foretaste of heaven. Many varieties of fantasy can undoubtedly be induced by hypnotic means. Detail of a fifth-century sarcophagus in the Archaeological Museum, Istanbul.

home town. This is a particularly valuable instance of our being able to see Jesus as a totally credible, flesh and blood figure.

So was Jesus just a clever first-century hypnotist? Certainly, quite aside from the cures, other incidents attributed to him lend themselves to this explanation. There is, for instance, his alleged first miracle, the changing of water into wine at Cana of Galilee, exclusively described in the narrative portion of the John gospel (John 2: 1-11). If we believe the water was actually turned into wine, then we must either accept it as a genuine miracle, or with the German theologians dismiss the story as a complete fabrication. But if we are prepared to accept that to those present the water *appeared* to have turned into wine, then hypnosis becomes not only possible but highly tenable as an explanation. As every stage hypnotist knows, it is one of the easiest and most entertaining of hypnotic demonstrations to suggest to a group of hypnotized volunteers that they are drinking some highly alcoholic (but in reality totally harmless) liquid, then watch them roll around the stage in comic states of 'inebriation'. With a set of genuinely inebriated guests at a wedding feast Jesus would have had an already highly suggestible group of subjects. And if it may be doubted that any state of hypnosis could be induced so speedily and so comprehensively, perhaps the explanation again lies in the degree of authority or awe commanded by the hypnotist. Peter Casson and other stage hypnotists claim virtually instantaneous results. Without even consciously using hypnosis, Rasputin gave some spectacular demonstrations of hypnotic power among the highly suggestible members of the court of pre-revolutionary Russia, not least in arresting the Tsar's son's haemophilia. Undoubtedly many people believed that God spoke and worked through Jesus. There can be little doubt that he believed this implicitly himself, and the very confidence this gave him could scarcely fail to impress the highly God-fearing people among whom he moved. Jesus clearly quite regarded healings and exorcisms as appropriate uses of the power that he possessed (Matthew 12: 28), and his need for disciples was in order to extend his powers as far as possible by sharing his work with them (Luke 9: 6).

This explanation for Jesus' miracles opens up something of a Pandora's box full of possible re-interpretations of the gospels. Since all sorts of illusions and fantasies can of course be induced by hypnosis, it is possible that the gospel accounts of the apparent 'transfiguration' - the incident in which, on a high mountain, Jesus is said to have turned into dazzling light before three disciples (Matthew 17: 1-8; Mark 9: 2-8; Luke 9: 28-36) - might have derived from nothing more than a hypnotic suggestion.

According to Dr Morton Smith, the initiation into the kingdom of God given to the secret gospel's young man at Gethsemane may have been a hypnotic fantasy 'trip' combined with instruction in hypnosis of the type Jesus had already given to most of the disciples. This would neatly correspond with the Mark gospel's otherwise cryptic words of Jesus to his closest associates: 'The secret of the kingdom of God is given to you, but to those who are outside everything comes in parables' (Mark 4: 11). It is also strikingly reminiscent of the fact, reported in Professor Gershom Scholem's *Major Trends in Jewish Mysticism*, that during the Middle Ages some Jews developed a technique of self-hypnosis which induced the experience of ascending into heaven and even sitting on the throne of God. Quite independently of any of Morton Smith's theories, it is common practice for most hypnotherapists to encourage their subjects to fantasize a beautiful beach or a garden. If Jesus indeed practised hypnosis, it is possible that he offered his disciples some not dissimilar foretaste of heaven. Morton Smith would interpret in this way the 'trip' Lazarus was sent on, his four days in the tomb being spent not in real death but in a death-like trance, all too easy to induce in hypnosis. It can even be done from a distance via post-hypnotic suggestion.

It is only right to set such a hypothesis in proper perspective. If whatever Jesus used to perform his healings, exorcisms and the like was indeed some form of hypnosis, there is not the slightest evidence that he used it for personal gain. In the case of his disciples' healings he instructed, 'You received without charge, give without charge' (Matthew 10: 8). The gospels emphasize Jesus' total disinclination to make any personal capital from his miracles. As we are told by the writer of John, the paralytic whom Jesus cured at the Sheep Pool did not even know who had cured him: 'The man had no idea who it was, since Jesus had disappeared into the crowd that filled the place' (John 5: 14). Equally importantly, even if all those diverse individuals to whom Jesus brought release from suffering were, in psychological terms, mere hysterics, the sheer scale of what Jesus managed to effect, and the spontaneity with which he is said to have achieved it, go far beyond what even the greatest braggadocio among hypnotists would profess to be able to achieve today.

There is a yet further, sombre, aspect of this issue. Had Jesus been just a clever hypnotist/exorcist he could no doubt have continued happily into old age making a comfortable living from his craft. But whatever Jesus' purpose was it was altogether more serious than this, as is apparent from the most well-attested feature of his life, the manner of his death.

WHY WAS HE KILLED?

IF Jesus was the unconventional, modernistic teacher and brilliant, selfless healer that he appears to have been, why was he killed? According to a succession of post-war writers, among them Manchester University's Professor S. G. F. Brandon and Jewish scholars Hyam Maccoby and Joel Carmichael, the answer is simple: Jesus' alleged pacifism was invented by the gospel writers in order to make him more acceptable to Gentiles. In reality he was an ardent Jewish nationalist in the mould of fellow Galilean Judas Galileus, who had staged the uprising against the Romans in 6 AD. Jesus' talk of the kingdom of God was an appeal for nothing less than the overthrow of the Romans and the establishment of a new, independent Jewish state. As represented by Joel Carmichael, Jesus' attempt to bring this about nearly succeeded. He managed to capture the Jerusalem Temple with 'an armed force powerful enough for him to seize this vast edifice and hold it for some time'. Equally, the gospel mention of the fall of the tower of Siloam (Luke 13: 4), was a reference to siege operations that the Romans were obliged to resort to in order to regain control of the city. The fact that Jesus' disciple Simon is specifically described as a Zealot (Luke 6: 15; Acts 1: 13; Mark 3: 19), is often quoted in support of such an argument, as is the Luke gospel report of Jesus recommending his disciples to arm themselves, just before his arrest in Gethsemane (Luke 22: 36–38).

Yet, as Dr Geza Vermes has commented, this portrayal of Jesus as some form of guerilla leader is far from convincing. Had he been involved in politics, we might at least have expected his utterances to be peppered with references to past historical events, such as Jerusalem's capture by Pompey, or Herod the Great's collaboration with the Romans, even if he avoided anything seditious on current affairs. But such subjects are simply not part of his vocabulary.

It seems clear, however, from one important episode referred to in the gospels – the entry into Jerusalem – that he was concerned with some form

Jesus rides into Jerusalem on a donkey (Matthew 21: 1-7), an action which clearly seems to have been provocative in intention. From the sarcophagus of Junius Bassus, city prefect of Rome, 359 AD. Vatican Museum, Rome.

Below Independent attestation of Pontius Pilate's governorship of Judaea is provided by this fragmentary inscription discovered at Caesarea in 1961. The text appears to read [CAESARIEN]S (IBUS) ... TIBERIEVM . . [PON]TIVS PILATVS [PRAEF]ECTVSIVDA[EA]E (To the people of Caesarea ... Tiberieum Pontius Pilate, Prefect of Judaea). This was apparently the dedicatory notice of a building Pilate erected in honour of his emperor, Tiberius. The inscription indicates that Pilate's correct title was 'prefect' rather than 'procurator', which was adopted some decades later.

of earthly kingship. In his time, just as today, Jerusalem was a holy city, the city of David, the city of the Temple to which every good Jew travelled at least once a year to make a sacrifice. Any pilgrim to Jerusalem was expected to make the final stages of the journey on foot as a sign of respect and devotion. Even as recently as 1917, when Britain's General Allenby took over the city from the Turks, he pointedly dismounted from his horse at the Jaffa Gate in deference to this tradition. Jesus, however, did the opposite. There are no references in the gospels to his using any form of animal transport in any other circumstances, but for his entry into Jerusalem he is described as going to elaborate lengths to procure a donkey and to be seen riding it into the city.

His choice of animal is particularly interesting. A horse would have seemed ostentatious, grandiose and militaristic. We might believe him to have had regal aspirations had he chosen a horse. But a donkey, then as now, could only be viewed as a humble beast. And there was another consideration. More than five hundred years earlier the *nabi* Zechariah had 'seen' the coming of the Messiah in precisely this manner:

> Shout with gladness, daughter of Jerusalem!
> See now, your king comes to you;
> He is victorious, he is triumphant,
> humble and riding on a donkey . . .
> He will proclaim peace for the nations.
> His empire will stretch from sea to sea . . .
> (Zechariah 9: 9–10)

Acclaiming Jesus on his entry, the gospels tell us, was a crowd waving palm branches and singing, 'Hosannah, blessed is he who comes in the name of the Lord', words from Psalm 118. As Canon Anthony Harvey has observed, this scene strongly recalls the triumphant purification and rededication of the Jerusalem Temple by the Hasmonean Simon Maccabeus after it had been defiled by Antiochus Epiphanes in the second century BC. During this episode, as described in the first book of Maccabees, 'The Jews made their entry . . . with acclamations and carrying palms . . . chanting hymns and canticles' (1 Maccabees 13: 51). If this *was* how Jesus entered Jerusalem, his gesture may be seen as aimed not at the Romans but at the Sadducean aristocracy. Their materialism, their lucrative concessions to money-changers and animal traders, and their concern only with the outward forms of religion made them the true defilers of the Temple. As support for this view, it was after his entry into Jerusalem that Jesus is described as embarking on his famous 'cleansing' of the Temple, knocking over the money-changers' tables, and driving out the animals and pigeons intended for sacrifice, in line with his repeated theme: What I want is mercy not sacrifice' (Matthew 9: 13 and elsewhere, after Hosea 6: 6).

It is descriptions of this episode which those who hold to the 'guerilla leader' view of Jesus regard as watered-down accounts of a full-scale insurrection led by him. Yet there is no serious case for interpreting his actions as anything more than the gesture that the gospels describe. Token though it may have been, however, backed by intelligence reports of the popular following Jesus had attracted, the gesture would have been more than sufficient to set alarm bells ringing in the affluent houses of the chief priests and other members of the Sadducean aristocracy. Sure enough, they were swiftly upon the scene. We are told that their first move was to question on what authority Jesus had behaved in such a manner, earning the characteristically cryptic reply: 'John's baptism, did it come from heaven, or from man?' (Mark 11: 30). It is a typical psychologist's device to answer a question with a question, and, as the gospels convey, Jesus frequently employed it himself, especially when someone tried to trap him. But of course, the real import of Jesus' response was its challenge to his questioners' authority. If they were prepared to acknowledge that John had been a mouthpiece of God, Jesus, as John's successor, could claim the same. Theoretically, then, harking back to the original concept of the *nabi*, the affairs of the Temple were for Jesus to command. Given the lifestyle of the men directing the Temple in Jesus' time, it is reasonable to assume that they would have been more than a little unwilling to relinquish their responsibilities, and the accompanying benefits, so lightly. The John gospel tells of a meeting of 'the chief priests and Pharisees' at which the argument ran:

> Here is this man working all these signs ... and what action are we taking? If we let him go on in this way everyone will believe in him ... (John 11: 47, 48)

Some present-day Jewish scholars have voiced doubts that Pharisees, who were very much of the people, would have connived with the aristocratic Sadducees against Jesus. There are good grounds for this thinking. Although Jesus is represented as frequently in dispute with the Pharisees, in Luke's gospel in particular there are several instances in which Pharisees entertain him socially and exhibit genuine concern for his safety (e.g. Luke 7: 36; 13: 31; 14: 1 and elsewhere). Those most consistently portrayed as contriving Jesus' death are the chief priests and scribes, who would have been Sadducees. Beyond doubt, however, at this point Jesus' days were numbered. A man with such popular support was a danger to the country's stability, and it is evident that an opportunity was eagerly sought to seize and silence him whenever it could be done with the least likelihood of opposition (Luke 19: 47, 48).

While his murder was being plotted, Jesus is described as spending the evening quietly with his disciples, having the meal now known as the Last Supper. The chronology of the John gospel, which tends to be more authoritative on such matters than the canonical gospels, suggests that this was not the Passover meal, or Seder, which had always to take place on the evening before the anniversary of the flight from Egypt. There are, however, a few clues that support the opposite view. We are told that there was wine on the table, indicating a celebration, and that to introduce the meal Jesus used the words of the Jewish Kiddush or Blessing, traditionally said by the head of a Jewish family before a Sabbath or on the eve of a major festival. The root of the Christian eucharist in this Jewish Kiddush is very obvious:

JEWISH KIDDUSH	CHRISTIAN EUCHARIST
Blessed are you, O Lord our God, King of the universe, who creates the fruit of the vine . . .	Blessed are you, Lord, God of all creation, through your goodness we have this wine to offer, fruit of the vine and work of human hands . . .
Blessed are you, O Lord our God, King of the universe, who brings forth bread from the earth.	Blessed are you, Lord, God of all creation, through your goodness we have this bread to offer, which earth has given and human hands have made.

The new element that we are told Jesus introduced into the rite at that meal is of course the identification of the bread and wine with the sacrifice of his own flesh and blood. Did he indeed see himself as the sacrificial victim that night, the divine response to Abraham's reputed willingness to offer his only son to God on the nearby Temple Mount, perhaps two thousand years before? As generally agreed by modern scholars, the offering of bread and wine was followed very, very swiftly by Jesus' crucifixion, and it has always been believed that this was the rite by which he specifically wished to be remembered. The first Christian eucharists were proper meals, the kind of occasion Jesus, in typical Jewish fashion, is said to have enjoyed to the full, descriptions of meals in general representing a high proportion of the gospels' content.

It seems strange perhaps that instead of Jesus and his disciples staying that night in the house where the meal took place, the gospels are unanimous

Jesus' 'last supper' with his disciples, as
depicted in a fresco from the third-century
Greek catacomb of Priscilla in Rome.
Instituting the rite commemorating his death,
Jesus used a formula of blessing deeply
rooted in Jewish religious tradition.

Right Jewish wooden eating bowls of the early
second century AD, found during the Bar-
Kokhba excavations; bowls such as these
would have been used at the 'last supper'.

in saying that the group went on to sleep in the garden of Gethsemane, on the outskirts of Jerusalem. But they also tell us that Jesus often met his disciples and stayed in the garden there with them overnight (John 18: 3; Luke 21: 37). Jerusalem's climate is equable, Jesus' following was large, and with thousands of other pilgrims gathered in the city for the festival, accommodation would inevitably have been limited. Many others were probably doing the same. Luke tells us that Jesus' group had two swords with them (Luke 22: 38), presumably essential protection in those circumstances. We know that even though the Essenes, like Jesus' followers, were required to travel with the absolute minimum, they were at least allowed 'weapons to keep off bandits' (Josephus *The Jewish War* Book II, 125).

The real mystery of the garden of Gethsemane episode lies in the extent to which Jesus did or did not know the fate in store for him that night. Did he, as argued in Hugh J. Schonfield's *Passover Plot*, actually plan that his treasurer disciple Judas Iscariot should betray him on this very night and at this particular spot, perhaps psychologically pressurizing Judas into such a move? Or, as has been argued by Dr Morton Smith, was Jesus' prime intention that night some form of baptismal initiation and indoctrination of the mysterious young man described exclusively by Mark as nearly captured in the garden on this occasion wearing 'nothing ... but a linen cloth' (Mark 14: 51), and identified in the secret gospel alone as Lazarus? Was this one of the occasions on which Jesus took a favoured disciple, through hypnosis, on a journey to the kingdom of God?

Either possibility is intriguing. That Jesus was that night in some fear for his life, and that someone else, while the main group of disciples slept, was close enough to observe this, would seem to be at least suggested by the information exclusive to Luke that 'in his anguish ... his sweat fell to the ground like great drops of blood' (Luke 22: 44). Considerable interest in this information has been expressed by forensic pathologist Dr Frederick Zugibe, chief medical examiner of Rockland County, New York. According to him the 'bloody sweat' strongly suggests a rare medical condition, haematidrosis, in which anything from one to thousands of subcutaneous blood vessels rupture into the exocrine sweat glands, causing the sufferer literally to 'sweat blood'. The condition is comparatively little known, and is invariably triggered by extreme emotional stress. That Jesus was observed to be displaying this symptom at the crisis time at Gethsemane, when he was *supposed* to be alone, gives us another of those tantalizing glimpses of him as a flesh and blood human being. It is tempting to believe, in accord with the Schonfield view, that he was intensely aware of the fatal path he had committed himself to, the ultimate in self-abnegation, and that there was no turning back. It is equally possible, and indeed not incompatible, that even on this crucial night he was conducting a baptismal indoctrination of the kind suggested by Dr Morton Smith, who has pointed out that in Spring a stream runs through Gethsemane.

Whatever Jesus' complex motives and emotions might have been that night, it is difficult to believe anything other than that he quite deliberately chose this particular time and place for his ultimate act of self-sacrifice. As represented in the gospels, while many of his followers, even though they had been sleeping, took the opportunity to slip away as the chink of armour heralded the approach of the arrest squad, Jesus stood his ground, at the same time forbidding resistance on the part of his companions.

So, we are told, that same night Jesus found himself on trial for his life before the very men whose conduct of religious affairs he had so outspokenly questioned. According to Mark and the other synoptic writers, the trial was conducted by 'the chief priests and the elders and the scribes ... the whole Sanhedrin' (Mark 14: 53–55). However, as has been pointed out very convincingly by most Jewish scholars, the historical authenticity of an overnight meeting on this occasion of the full Sanhedrin, the supreme Jewish council, is extremely doubtful. No normal Sanhedrin meeting ever took place at night, and the difficulties of summoning appropriate representatives from their beds at festival time would have been far greater than simply holding Jesus overnight, or indeed over several nights had there been any legitimate trial. Significantly, the John gospel, which we have learnt to trust on narrative matters, merely refers to Jesus being shuttled between two high priestly houses, those of Caiaphas and his father-in-law, Annas, two men with the most to lose if Jesus' popularity went unchecked. Although the house of Caiaphas has not yet been identified in Israeli excavations of old Jerusalem, it is thought by some to have been one of the imposing edifices on the Akra, the former hill fortress south-west of the Temple Mount.

It seems likely, then, that Jesus' 'trial' was in fact little more than a hasty overnight interrogation by two Sadducees motivated by self-interest rather than a desire for justice. What, therefore, are we to believe of the charges on which Jesus is said to have been condemned? Mark's gospel represents the high priest as asking Jesus: 'Are you the Messiah, the Son of the Blessed One?' (Mark 14: 61). When Jesus gives an affirmative answer the high priest tears his robes in apparent despair at such blasphemy. The John gospel says the charge on which the priests brought Jesus before Pilate for execution was 'because he has claimed to be the Son of God' (John 19: 7). But, as modern Jewish scholars have pointed out, the problem with this description of events, however familiar it may be to generations of Christians, is that it is simply incompatible with what is known of contemporary Jewish thought. It was not an offence for any Jew to claim to be the Messiah as such because someone, some time, had to be he. As the Jewish *Midrash* notes, at the time of the Second Jewish Revolt of 132 AD, the great Rabbi Akiba specifically acclaimed rebel leader Simon Bar-Kokhba with the words: 'This is the king Messiah!' Akiba's companion is reported to have scoffed: 'Akiba, grass will grow in your jawbones and he will still not have come!' But the claim as such was no offence.

Even more implausible is the high priest's apparent automatic association of the title 'Messiah' with a claim to be *the* Son of God. Certainly the title was associated with a claim to be *a* son of God, and Jesus would automatically have been considered the man most deserving of such an appellation. The association is made in Psalm 2, for instance, and in some Dead Sea Scroll references. But no high priest would have made the connection in the divine terms in which it is couched in the gospels, because the Jews did not conceive of the Messiah as divine. It needs to be stressed, furthermore, that the claim to be 'Son of God' was again no offence in itself. In the words of Rabbi Morris Goldstein:

> Use of the phrase 'Son of the Blessed' or 'Son of God' was no capital crime . . . no, not in Mishnah, nor in pre-Mishnah law; it is an expression found often in apocalyptic literature. The reference to sitting at the right hand of *Power* (Mark 14: 62) is not greatly different from King David's allusion to himself as sitting at the right hand of God (Psalm 110: 1); at all events, it is nowhere indicated as blasphemy.

Further doubt about the overall accuracy of the gospels in reporting these events (which occurred, after all, when Jesus' followers were either absent or in considerable disarray), arises from Jesus' inquisitors being said to have handed him over to Pilate because: 'We are not allowed to put a man to death' (John 18: 31). The unlikelihood of this is evident from the fact that the book of Acts describes the martyr Stephen being stoned by the Jerusalem Sanhedrin for an apparently similar blasphemy (Acts: 7: 59–60) shortly after Jesus' death. Although some have argued that this was a mere mob lynching, it is clear that the Temple authorities had at least some power of execution, most likely reserved for special offences against the Temple, from archaeological discovery of the incised stone notices warning of the death penalty for any Gentile daring to trespass into the Temple's exclusively Jewish areas. A near complete example of these notices is in the Archaeological

Museum at Istanbul, another, more fragmentary, is in Jerusalem's Rockefeller Museum (see p 153). So there seems little doubt that the high priests could there and then have publicly killed Jesus had they felt they were acting with the full approval of the Jewish people. There is every reason to suppose, however, that they would have been extremely unpopular had they done so, and it must have seemed much more expedient to have the Roman governor Pilate do the job for them. He had come to Jerusalem to keep an eye on events during Passover (he was normally based at Caesarea), and he was militarily equipped to deal with any disturbance.

There can be no question that Pontius Pilate once existed. In 1961 a Roman dedicatory inscription bearing his name as *praefectus* of Judaea was found at Caesarea in the ruins of a temple that he is thought to have built in honour of Tiberius (see p 115). Pilate is also mentioned at some length in the writings of Josephus, in connection with his attempted suppression of two remarkable demonstrations of Jewish passive resistance. In one, having offended Jewish religious scruples by displaying his legion's image-bearing standards in Jerusalem, he found himself beset by an 'angry city mob ... joined by a huge influx of people from the country', who surrounded his Caesarea home, imploring him to remove the offending objects. When Pilate refused, as Josephus relates, this entire crowd 'fell prone all round his house and remained motionless for five days and nights'. Pilate, concerned to rid himself of this nuisance, had the gathering surrounded by a ring of soldiers three deep, who advanced with drawn swords. But at this, according to Josephus:

> ... the Jews as though by agreement fell to the ground in a body and bent their necks, shouting that they were ready to be killed rather than transgress the Law. Amazed at the intensity of their fervour Pilate ordered the standards to be removed from Jerusalem forthwith.

In the case of the second demonstration, against his use of some of the Temple tax for the building of an aqueduct, Pilate was more cunning. He had his soldiers '... mix with the mob, wearing civilian clothing over their armour, and with orders not to draw their swords but to use clubs on the obstreperous.' This method he appears to have found more effective: '... many died from the blows, and many were trampled on by their friends as they fled.'

The interest value of these episodes is threefold. First, the standards incident in particular is a fascinating indication, quite independent of anything in the gospels, of the deployment in Jesus' time of Jewish passive resistance methods that Mahatma Gandhi would have been proud of. Although we are told nothing of the leader or leaders of those who bared their necks to Pilate's soldiers, their actions accord unerringly with the message of the man who taught: 'offer the wicked man no resistance ... if anyone hits you on the right cheek, offer him the other as well' (Matthew 5: 38).

Secondly, the same two incidents are mentioned by Josephus in his book *Antiquities* immediately before the reference to Jesus discussed in chapter three. This reference is acknowledged to have been altered later, and Paul Winter and others have noted that it appears to be incomplete. Did Josephus directly link Jesus with some third popular demonstration in terms medieval Christian copyists felt obliged to suppress? Could this have been the incident Luke's gospel hints at:

> It was just about this time that some people arrived and told him [Jesus] about the Galileans whose blood Pilate had mingled with that of their sacrifices. (Luke 13: 1)

Is there some significance in Mark's cryptic reference to Barabbas as one who had been thrown into prison 'with the rioters who had committed murder during the uprising' (Mark 15: 7)? Whatever was suppressed is unlikely to have been earth-shattering, or we would have heard about it from those commentators on Josephus, such as Origen, who were writing before the text was mutilated. But there is a suspicion that Jesus, albeit passively, had stirred up greater popular Jewish fervour than the Gentile gospels convey.

The third point of interest is Pilate's reaction to the passive resistance methods. He acts neither as the insensitive butcher some modern authors have tried to label him, nor as the pusillanimous capitulator to mob demands portrayed by the gospel writers. A man clearly used to the ways of violence – he was, after all, regionally responsible for the world's most efficient fighting machine, the Roman army – he nonetheless exhibits a superstitious awe of individuals ready to lay down their lives for what to him would have seemed trifling religious niceties. It is possible that he genuinely raised some objection to putting Jesus to death just to satisfy the demands of the Sadducean high priesthood. The gospels refer to a Jewish crowd positively baying for Jesus' blood when Pilate suggested he might be spared. With considerable justification, many writers have remarked that if this was a representative Jewish crowd, it is strange that their attitude should have changed so markedly from the effusive welcome they had given Jesus on his

Roman crucifixion was viewed with such horror that
conventional artists refrained from depicting it. The
only surviving contemporary representations derive
from graffiti and a magical gem: *Above* Graffito from
Pozzuoli, near Naples, showing victim crucified with
knees apart. Contrary to popular Christian depictions,
he appears to be facing the cross (see also frontispiece).
Right Magical gem, formerly in the Pereire collection.
In this example the attitude is unmistakably face
outwards, but as in the Pozzuoli graffito, the knees are
wide apart.

arrival in Jerusalem. The most likely explanation – assuming, of course, there ever was such a crowd – is that they were a carefully orchestrated gathering of the Sadducees' own paid employees. After all, with twenty thousand Temple servants and eighteen thousand workmen on their payroll, the Temple's controllers would scarcely have had any difficulty in finding a mob to perform to whatever tune they called. Another possible explanation, however, is that Jesus was indeed disowned by those who had welcomed him to Jerusalem – because he had failed to sanction the abortive uprising against the Romans that arguably they had launched in his name. If the latter was the case, it would inevitably have been accompanied by disillusionment, and bitterness against Jesus as a betrayer of those who had given their lives in his cause. After all, Honi the Circle Drawer was stoned to death for refusing to curse an unpopular politician and his party. Whatever the true circumstances, the only reliable information we have, independent of the gospels, is Josephus' bald statement, 'Upon an indictment by leading members of our society, Pilate sentenced him to the cross'.

Of the exact details of the crucifixion itself the gospel writers seem to have been concerned to spare their readers the more harrowing details, and small wonder. This barbaric method of execution, earlier employed by Scythians, Assyrians and Carthaginians – none of them the most squeamish of people – was universally execrated as a form of punishment, and, among the Romans, reserved only for slaves and foreign rebels against the state. Undoubtedly because crucifixion was so abhorred, only the scantiest of contemporary information about it has survived, most of this in the form of a handful of artistic representations. Two of these are crude graffiti, one from Pozzuoli, just outside Naples, the other from the Palatine Hill, near Rome. Two others are tiny depictions on gems, one example (see p 125) being from the Pereire Collection in Paris. Although many thousands were crucified during the Roman era – in 71 BC alone the Roman consul Crassus had six thousand rebels of the Spartacus uprising strung up along Italy's Via Appia – there has been a marked dearth of skeletal remains identifiable as those of crucifixion victims. One of the reasons for this seems to have been a medical black market for crucifixion nails in antiquity. They were thought to be effective against bee-stings, fevers and epilepsy, for example, and they could be withdrawn from the body leaving no identifiable trace of the cause of death.

In 1968, however, in the course of the Giv'at ha-Mivtar excavations, one of the ossuaries examined was found to contain an adult skeleton, the two heel bones of which were securely joined together by a nail nearly 17 cm long. The ossuary's inscription identified this individual as one 'Jehohanan',

Crucifixion nail transfixing the heel bones of victim excavated at Giv'at ha-Mivtar. Traces of wood were found either side of the bones, and a number of theories have been put forward to explain their exact origins, particles of acacia being thought to derive from the *titulus*, or notice of crime, and olive wood from the cross upright – though it has been pointed out that olive would have been particularly unsuitable for cross-making. The olive wood may therefore derive from a foot platform, which might also explain the bent nail.

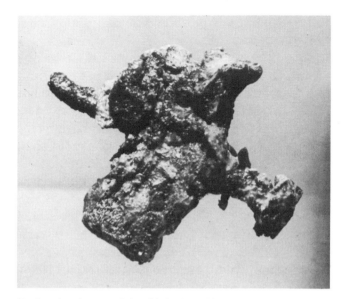

Broken leg-bones of the Giv'at ha-Mivtar crucifixion victim. These provide the most explicit corroboration of the John gospel information that it was standard practice for Jewish crucifixion victims to have their legs broken (John 19: 31–4). The purpose of leg-breaking would seem to have been to prevent the victim pushing himself up for breath, thereby causing him to die of asphyxia. Outside the Jewish world crucifixion victims could survive for three days or more (see p 130).

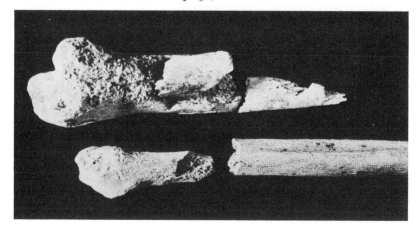

and it is evident from the skeletal remains that he was a gracefully built, cleft-palated male in his mid-twenties, who undoubtedly died of crucifixion. Among both Christians and Jews the discovery has raised lively interest, and no little controversy, as to the exact form the crucifixion took. Even the Israeli anatomist who conducted the main forensic examination, Dr Nicu Haas of the Hebrew University's Hadassah Medical School, acknowledged some uncertainty. He suggested two possible positions in which the man might have been crucified, one with the legs forced into an awkward side-saddle position, the other with the knees apart. Haas finally favoured the side-saddle suggestion, but since the publication of his report the renowned Israeli archaeologist Dr Yigael Yadin, well known as the excavator of Masada, has expressed his support for the alternative position, with the knees apart. According to Yadin, although the ossuary's inscription is difficult to decipher, it may well read: 'Jehohanan ... the one hanged with his knees apart.' Such a position certainly corresponds with the Pozzuoli graffito and the Pereire Collection gem. Another possible reconstruction has come from the Copenhagen Medical Museum specialist Dr Møller Christensen. From traces of wood on both sides of Jehohanan's ankles, he has deduced that the feet have been forced into a crude wooden frame, and then locked in with a transverse nail.

Of course, whatever the exact method used for Jehohanan, Jesus was not necessarily crucified the same way. Crucifixion procedures are known to have varied; for instance, the disciple Peter was reputedly crucified upside down. But there is one feature of Dr Nicu Haas' observations on Jehohanan's skeleton which has a particular importance in suggesting that the gospels are, at least to some extent eyewitness accounts. As noted by Dr Haas:

The right tibia and the left calf bones (tibia and fibula) were all broken in their last third at the same level, but in a different manner: the right tibia had brutally been fractured, by comminution, into sharp slivers; the left tibia and fibula were broken by a simple, oblique, dentate-serrate line. Both types of fractures are characteristic in fresh bone. The fracture of the right tibial bone (the fibula being unavailable for study), was produced by a single, strong blow. This direct, deliberate blow may be attributed to the final 'coup de grace'.

Essentially, Jehohanan had his legs savagely smashed. One is immediately reminded of the breaking of the legs of Jesus' two crucifixion companions, as exclusively reported in the John gospel:

... to prevent the bodies remaining on the cross during the sabbath ... the Jews asked Pilate to have the legs broken and the bodies taken away. Consequently the soldiers came and broke the legs of the first man who had been crucified with him

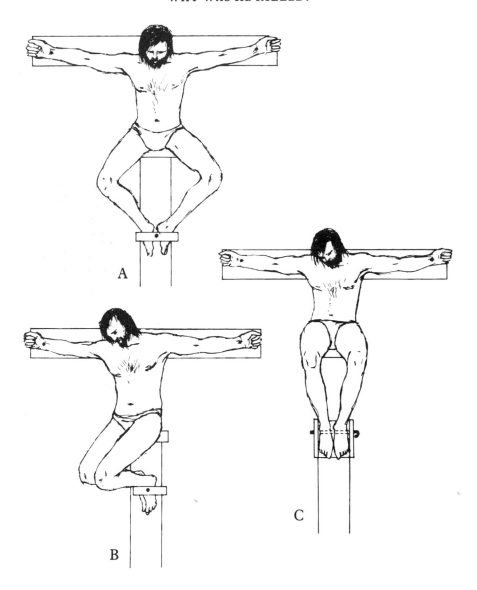

Reconstructions of the crucifixion attitude of the Giv'at ha-Mivtar victim: A, the 'knees apart' attitude first advanced by the late Dr Nicu Haas; B, 'side-saddle' posture subsequently favoured by Dr Haas; C, knees apart, with foot-platform arrangement, as reconstructed by Dr Møller Christensen. These alternatives by no means exhaust the possibilities – upside-down and face-inwards variants have also been suggested. The gospels provide no information on Jesus' crucifixion attitude, and the concept that he was nailed to a cross is only to be gleaned by inference from John 20: 25.

and then of the other. When they came to Jesus they found he was already dead, and so instead of breaking his legs one of the soldiers pierced his side with a lance ... (John 19: 31–34)

The important feature here is that the 'breaking of the legs' was a procedure carried out only on Jewish crucifixion victims. In other countries victims would be left on the cross during the night, and it might take up to three days for them to expire. But in a Jewish milieu, because it was against the Mosaic Law for a body to be left on a cross after sundown, the legs were broken to hasten death. John's report appears, therefore, to provide an authentic detail of which a Gentile writer, working from a distance, could not be expected to have been aware. To the old German theologians the 'breaking of the legs' was interpreted as most likely an invention by the gospel writer in order to make the fact that Jesus escaped this treatment correspond with Jewish requirements concerning the paschal lamb, 'nor must you break any bone of it' (Exodus 12: 46) and the Messianic prophecy of Psalm 34: 20, 'God rescues him ... Taking care of every bone ... God will not let one be broken'. Modern archaeology proves them wrong and gives further justification for believing that at least the narrative content of the John gospel contains some authentic, eyewitness detail. John claims this reliability for himself in respect of another crucifixion detail, the physiological effects of the lance reportedly thrust into Jesus' side:

... immediately there came out blood and water. This is the evidence of one who saw it – trustworthy evidence, and he knows he speaks the truth ... (John 19: 34, 35).

As reported in all the canonical gospels, the final act of the crucifixion saga was the arrival on the scene, after Jesus' death, of a mysterious secret disciple, a 'rich man' called Joseph of Arimathea, who took charge of Jesus' body. Why such a man should have emerged only at this moment, and, conversely, why not a single one of Jesus' closest associates appears to have lifted a finger to organize some form of burial it is impossible to know in the present state of the evidence. Hugh Schonfield, in *The Passover Plot*, has suggested that this detail, like the provision of the donkey for the entry, was one carefully pre-arranged by Jesus, and there is much to be said for at least this aspect of Schonfield's theories. Jesus' family background was almost certainly not as poor as popularly supposed; it is clear that some of his friends were wealthy and influential people, and that he was quite prepared to accept their help whenever circumstance demanded – hence the provision, for instance, of the Jerusalem house for the Last Supper.

Joseph, we are told, provided the grave linen and spices for the burial, and the tomb itself. Normally a Jew would have been buried in his sabbath-best clothes, but Jesus had had his clothes removed at the time of the crucifixion, the garments being shared out as part of the pickings by the execution squad, and Joseph is described as purchasing a length of linen in which to wrap the otherwise naked corpse. Such a piece of linen would normally be expected to have mouldered away long ago, but preserved in the Cathedral of Turin is a fourteen-foot length of linen, bearing apparent imprints of the back and front of a naked, crucified body, which is claimed to be the very cloth in which Jesus of Nazareth was wrapped. The cloth at Turin certainly dates from the Middle Ages at least. Dust particles in the linen have been found to include pollen grains from plants of undoubted Near Eastern provenance, and, most impressively, when viewed in negative the body and facial imprints take on an astonishingly lifelike quality. Together with what appear to be blood stains, these imprints have led several pathologists to contend that the cloth did at least wrap the body of someone crucified in manner identical to that recorded of Jesus. The apparent bloodstains suggest that the body was not washed before burial and this has led some to argue that the Shroud cannot be authentic because the Jewish rite always included washing. However, as recently pointed out by London University Jewish scholar Victor Tunkel, if a first-century Jew died a bloody death, such as from crucifixion, the body would quite specifically not have been washed, in order to keep the life-blood with the body in preparation for the anticipated physical resurrection – striking evidence in favour of the Shroud's authentic Jewishness. Other aspects of the case for and against the Shroud's authenticity have been argued at length elsewhere, by the present author among others, but intriguing as this object is, ultimately only radio-carbon dating, yet to be carried out, can provide a positive assurance that the linen genuinely dates from the first century. Even then we are a long way from proving that the man of the Shroud was actually Jesus. The evidence for his identity finally has to be sought by other means. One fascinating feature of the Shroud, in the context of Dr Morton Smith's theories on Jesus' baptismal initiation rite, should, however, be pointed out. Dr Smith suggests that the rich young man of the 'secret gospel' was given his initiation into the 'kingdom of heaven' by being 'buried', wrapped up naked for three days in a single sheet. If the Shroud is genuine, it looks as if Jesus' burial took an almost identical form, with his naked body wrapped in a linen sheet in the darkness of a tomb. In Jesus' case, however, the death was not acted out but real.

If the Shroud is one possible tangible link with the historical Jesus,

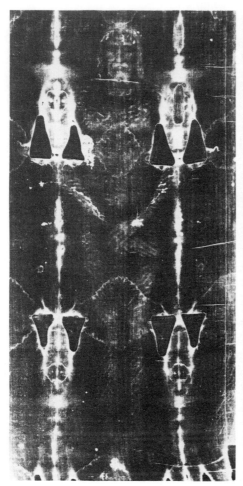

Above The Turin Shroud, showing frontal view of crucified body in negative. According to some, this is the very cloth which wrapped Jesus in the tomb and was imprinted with his death image. According to others it is a clever medieval forgery.

Right Interior of tomb of the time of Jesus at Giv'at ha-Mivtar near Jerusalem. Normal Jewish practice was for the body to be laid out to decompose, and later for the bones to be gathered up into an ossuary, or bone box.

another, also associated with Joseph of Arimathea, may be the tomb in which he was laid. The gospels describe Joseph as having laid Jesus in his own new, rock-cut tomb 'in which no-one had yet been buried' (John 19: 41). Perhaps significantly, the tomb is described as having been in a garden, close to Golgotha (John 19: 41–42). The information that the tomb was one 'in which no-one had yet been buried' might appear puzzling but the implication that graves were re-used is absolutely consistent with the information yielded by excavated Jewish burials of the time of Jesus. As was found during the excavations at Giv'at ha-Mivtar, a single tomb might contain not only one or more 'laying-out' places, but perhaps eight or nine chambers cut into the rock to accommodate ossuaries, the stone boxes in which the bones were gathered once the corpse had decomposed. Since each chamber might accommodate two or three ossuaries, and each ossuary might be used for two or more sets of bones, a single tomb might accumulate some twenty or thirty different interments over a period of several decades. So Jesus would have been rarely privileged to be laid in a tomb 'in which no-one had yet been buried'. This provides an element of authentic Jewish detail in that, for the Romans and other Gentiles, cremation was the norm.

The traditional site for Jesus' tomb is marked today by Jerusalem's Church of the Holy Sepulchre, a bewildering rabbit warren of an edifice with a type of mausoleum, obviously not original, in its depths, which houses a carefully protected stone slab on which Jesus' body is reputed to have been laid. It has been identified as Jesus' burial place at least since the time when Helena, mother of Constantine the Great, reputedly 'discovered' it back in the fourth century AD, in circumstances described by the near-contemporary church historian Socrates Scholasticus:

Helena went to Jerusalem, to find what had been that city as desolate as 'a lodge in a garden of cucumbers' ... after the Passion Christians paid great devotion to Christ's tomb, but those who hated Christianity covered the spot with a mound of earth, built a temple of Aphrodite on it, and set up her statue there, so that the place would be forgotten. The device was successful for a long time – until, in fact, it became known to the Emperor's [i.e. Constantine the Great's] mother. She had the statue thrown down, the earth removed and the site cleared, and found three crosses in the tomb ... With them was also found the *titulum* on which Pilate had written in various languages that the Christ crucified was the king of the Jews ...

From one of the three crosses found by Helena came most of the pieces of the 'True Cross' venerated in numerous churches and cathedrals throughout the world. The *titulus* is still to be seen in Rome's Basilica of Santa Croce in Gerusalemme, a puzzling piece of work with an inscription just decipherable

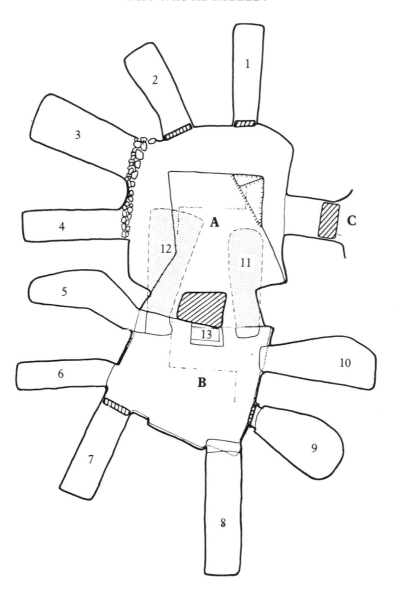

'. . . a new tomb, in which no-one had yet been buried' (John 19: 41). Archaeological excavations at Jewish burial sites such as Jericho and Giv'at ha-Mivtar reveal that it was common practice for a single rock-cut tomb to have a series of burial niches, or loculi, into each of which would be placed one or more ossuaries. Jesus would therefore have been specially privileged to be laid in an unused tomb. The ground plan above is from tomb I at Giv'at ha-Mivtar, which had two chambers on different levels, each with loculi leading off.

as 'Jesus the Nazarene, King of the Jews', written in Aramaic, Greek and Latin (see John 19: 19). Somewhat unconvincingly, the Greek and Latin have been written from right to left in the manner normal for Aramaic. Most likely this is a piece of sharp fourth-century forgery, as are the pieces of the cross in all probability, but there may be a case, in view of the marking of the spot with the Temple of Aphrodite (built by the Emperor Hadrian), for accepting the location of the tomb itself as being the one in which Jesus' body was laid. According to the gospels the tomb was outside Jerusalem's walls, but by Helena's time the walls had been rebuilt centuries before and the tomb was inside them. There must, therefore, have been something compelling about the site for her to ignore the gospels' descriptions. As archaeologist Dr Kathleen Kenyon has discovered, the tomb found by Helena *was* outside the city walls of Jesus' time. At that point it seems to have been a quarry used for burials, and Armenian archaeologists have very recently unearthed another well-preserved tomb close to the one attributed to Jesus. Sadly, Helena's son Constantine so altered the tomb's original appearance by grandiose building projects, which in turn became the subject of repeated Moslem attacks, that today almost every vestige of the original has been lost. Understandably visitors turn to the more impressive 'Garden Tomb' to see what Jesus' burial place might have looked like, and General Gordon of Khartoum suggested that this was indeed the actual tomb of Jesus, though there is very little evidence to support his theory. In any case, as with the Turin Shroud, perhaps the inevitable reaction to such relics is 'so what?' The real issue is that Jesus was, to all appearances, dead when laid in Joseph of Arimathea's tomb, and that this was not the end of the story.

THE EMPTY TOMB
MYSTERY

ACCORDING to every available early source, Jesus died on the cross at the hands of the world's most efficient executioners, the Romans. The Roman governor is reported to have sent a senior officer to ensure, before the body was taken down from the cross, that Jesus was actually dead (Mark 15: 45). Leaving nothing to chance, a lance was plunged into his chest, as observed in the John gospel, and blood and a watery fluid oozed out. The apparently lifeless body was then laid out in a tomb not far from the execution site.

Yet, two days later, not only had the body mysteriously disappeared but people who had known Jesus well began to have strange experiences of seeing him among them. Sometimes distrusting their own senses, they reported seeing him pass through locked doors, yet he was able to talk and eat with them (Luke 24: 43), and he even felt like a living person to the touch (John 20: 27, 28). The convincing nature of these encounters to those involved is conveyed by the speech attributed to Peter in the tenth chapter of Acts:

Now I, and those with me, can witness to everything he did throughout the countryside of Judaea and in Jerusalem itself: and also to the fact that they killed him by hanging him on a tree, yet three days afterwards God raised him to life and allowed him to be seen, not by the whole people, but only by certain witnesses God had chosen beforehand. Now we are those witnesses – we have eaten and drunk with him after his resurrection from the dead ... (Acts 10: 39–42)

It is generally acknowledged, even by the 'Jesus did not exist' exponent, Professor G. A. Wells, that this belief took hold soon after the events described, and that at least one believer, the apostle Paul, can be reliably dated. In Acts 18: 12 Paul is said to have appeared before the Achaean proconsul Gallio during his second mission. Gallio's administration is accurately dateable to the years 51–2 AD. from an inscription discovered at Delphi, and from this it can be calculated that Paul must have believed in

Jesus' resurrection *c.* 40 AD, and perhaps, according to some authorities, as early as 36 AD. So what had happened to account for the fact that Paul and others held this belief? In this ostensibly simple question lies the central mystery of the Christian religion, and one for which there remains no uncontested rational answer.

The various accounts of the scene at the empty tomb on the first Easter morning are so full of inconsistencies that it is easy to deride them. The writer of the John gospel describes Mary Magdalen arriving at the tomb alone, discovering the tomb to be empty and imparting the news to Peter and an unnamed 'other disciple, the one Jesus loved' (John 20: 2). The Matthew author relates that Mary Magdalen was accompanied by 'Mary the mother of James and Joseph'. Mark adds a further companion, a woman called Salome, referred to in the Thomas gospel. Luke, who knows nothing of any Salome, speaks only of one 'Joanna', together with other women who go off to tell the disciples what they have seen, but according to Mark the women, 'frightened out of their wits . . . said nothing to a soul, for they were afraid' (Mark 16: 8).

Similar discrepancies occur in reports of what was seen at the empty tomb. John's Mary Magdalen saw first two angels sitting in the tomb and then Jesus, whom she was not allowed to touch. Matthew's two Marys saw one seated angel, and then Jesus. Mark's three women saw a young man in a white robe, and Mary Magdalen alone saw Jesus. Luke's group of women saw two men in brilliant clothes who suddenly appeared at their side, but not Jesus himself, who was seen only by two disciples on the road to Emmaus. All four gospels describe Jesus subsequently appearing to the full group of disciples, but while Matthew and Mark set these appearances in Galilee, the Luke and John gospels suggest that the setting was Jerusalem. Luke also indirectly mentions an earlier appearance of Jesus to Simon Peter, one which seems to have gone unnoticed elsewhere in the gospels. But it is one of Paul's letters which gives the fullest information of all:

> . . . he [Jesus] appeared first to Cephas [Peter] and secondly to the Twelve. Next he appeared to more than five hundred of the brothers at the same time, most of whom are still alive, though some have died; then he appeared to James and then to all the apostles; and last of all he appeared to me too . . . (1 Corinthians 15: 5–8)

The documentation is an almost hopeless jumble of confusion, scarcely helped by the fact that the ever enigmatic Mary Magdalen, the only witness mentioned in every account except Paul's – for whom women didn't count – was obviously so unbalanced that she had needed to be cured by Jesus of 'seven devils'. The lack of a proper ending to the Mark gospel, as revealed by the *Sinaiticus* and *Vaticanus* manuscripts, merely adds to the problem. Yet had someone wholly invented the resurrection story one might have expected them to do so more convincingly than, for instance, representing women as the prime witnesses, when women's testimony carried a particularly low weight in Jewish law. And in their own way the garblings and inconsistencies have the same quality as the memories of witnesses after a road accident, which are, after all, personal and often highly confused versions of the same true story.

Any number of theories have been advanced in an attempt to explain what really happened, but all may be reduced to permutations of six basic hypotheses:

1 The women went to the wrong tomb.

2 Unknown to the disciples, some independent person removed the body.

3 The disciples themselves removed the body and invented the whole story.

4 The disciples saw not the real Jesus, but hallucinations.

5 Jesus did not actually die on the cross, but was resuscitated, or in some other way survived.

6 Jesus really did rise from the grave.

It is impossible within a single chapter to do justice to these different hypotheses, but it is clear that the disciples and gospel writers anticipated that the first four theories would be proposed to explain the mystery. All the synoptic writers emphasize, for instance, how the women had carefully taken note of where Jesus was laid (Matthew 27: 61; Mark 15: 47; Luke 23: 55). The John gospel puts into the mind of Mary Magdalen the idea that the man she mistook for a gardener (in reality Jesus, as yet unrecognized) had for some reason taken the body away (John 20: 15). The writer of Matthew acknowledges that in his time there was a story in circulation that the disciples had stolen the body. He accuses 'the Jews' of having bribed the guards posted at Jesus' tomb to say this. Both the Luke and John gospels emphasize the disciples' own incredulity that what they were seeing was more than an apparition: Luke wonderingly reports '... they offered him a piece of fish which he took and ate before their eyes' (Luke 24: 43) and John relates that the disciple Thomas insisted that he was not prepared to believe unless he was able to put his fingers into the wound in Jesus' side, which he was allowed to do.

Perhaps because the gospel writers do not take account of it, the fifth hypothesis, that Jesus did not die on the cross, has been particularly favoured by sceptics in recent years. In *The Passover Plot* Hugh J. Schonfield advanced the ingenious theory that the sponge offered to Jesus on the cross (John 19: 29, 30) was soaked not in vinegar but in a drug to induce the appearance of death. This was so that he could be taken to the tomb by Joseph of Arimathea and there resuscitated, but the lance thrust into Jesus' side by the Romans caused the plot to misfire. According to Schonfield, the man seen by Mary Magdalen was simply someone who had been deputed to help revive Jesus, and the 'resurrection' was therefore nothing more than a case of mistaken identity, Jesus' body having been quietly buried elsewhere. There have been all sorts of versions of this theory. In D.H. Lawrence's short story 'The Man Who Died', Jesus was taken down too early from the cross, revived in the tomb, petrified his followers, who assumed he was dead, 'resurrected', and then slipped away to Egypt to enjoy conjugal relations with a priestess of Isis. The supposedly factual *The Holy Blood and the Holy Grail* by Baigent, Leigh and Lincoln represents Jesus' paramour as Mary Magdalen and their place of refuge as the South of France, but it follows essentially the same plot.

Today's Ahmadiya Muslims, only a little less fancifully, claim that Jesus even managed to get as far as India, and at Srinagar, Kashmir, visitors are shown a shrine purported to be his true tomb. The problem of all such hypotheses, certainly those postulating some form of resuscitation, was outlined more than a hundred years ago by the controversial Tübingen lecturer David Strauss, one of those nineteenth-century German theologians who in so many ways cast doubts on the gospel story. As Strauss wrote in his *New Life of Jesus*, published in 1865:

> It is impossible that a being who had stolen half dead out of the sepulchre, who crept about weak and ill, wanting medical treatment, who required bandaging, strengthening and indulgence ... could have given the disciples the impression that he was a Conqueror over death and the grave, the Prince of Life, an impression which lay at the bottom of their future ministry. Such a resuscitation ... could by no possibility have changed their sorrow into enthusiasm, have elevated their reverence into worship!

At the beginning of this century a group of German scholars, the History of Religion School, whose most prominent members included Richard Reitzenstein and Wilhelm Bousset, pointed out the remarkable similarity between Jesus' death and resurrection and the old pagan concept of a dying and resurrected fertility god, as briefly mentioned in chapter four. The cults of Adonis, Osiris, Tammuz and others – the names varied from one country to another – were still prevalent in the first century AD. As winter brought death to crops and vegetation, all over the Near East women mourned the god's death at special tomb shrines. Then, at the break of spring, as trees came into leaf, and new vegetation appeared, there was rejoicing that the god had risen from the dead. Festive processions were held, with palms, fans, and even symbolic eggs, precursors of Christianity's familiar Easter eggs.

It must be remembered that Galilee had been pagan until the second century BC, and only became forcibly converted to the Jewish religion during the Hasmonean period that followed the Maccabean revolt. It is very probable that among ordinary people of Jesus' time there lingered superstitious hankerings for the old myth of the dying and resurrected god, just as in the West old superstitions and witch-cults persisted long after the introduction of Christianity. But as a consensus of modern scholars have pointed out, the Christian story of death and resurrection is really quite different from the symbolism of the crop cycle which lies at the heart of the old fertility religions. On close inspection the parallels are unimpressive, and contrary to the view that anyone was expecting Jesus' resurrection the gospels stress the women's fear and astonishment at his post-crucifixion appearances.

If the hypothesis that Jesus did rise from the grave is set aside as being impossible to prove, the only remaining theory meriting further consideration is that the disciples somehow hallucinated Jesus' resurrection appearances. The gospel writers stress his tangibility, and some modern commentators have argued particularly forcefully against the hallucination hypothesis. Nonetheless, in view of Jesus' powers of hypnosis, discussed in chapter six, it is possible that he prepared his disciples for his resurrection using the technique that modern hypnotists call post-hypnotic suggestion. By this means he could have effectively conditioned them to hallucinate his appearances in response to certain pre-arranged cues (the breaking of bread?), for a predetermined period after his death. Using hypnotic suggestion a subject can be persuaded to see, hear, feel, even smell an imaginary person, and then to reproduce these sensations, given an appropriate trigger, long after being woken from hypnosis. A particularly striking experiment of this kind, conducted for the purposes of a BBC television programme, has been described by the author Colin Wilson:

A volunteer – a housewife who was known to be a good hypnotic subject – was placed under hypnosis by a doctor. She was told that when she awakened she would be taken to another place where I (Colin Wilson) would approach her (followed by a television camera). As I spoke to her she would 'see' the sinister figure of a seventeenth-century clergyman standing nearby; the man's appearance was described in detail. She was awakened and taken to the Bristol Docks, where I was waiting. As I walked towards her she smiled at me, then her eyes strayed across the water to an abandoned wharf. Her smile vanished and she asked me with amazement,

'Where did he go?'

'Who?'

'That man.'

She pointed to the dock and described the unpleasant, sallow-looking man dressed in old-fashioned clothes who had been standing on the wharf, then vanished. Even when the hypnotist explained that she had been responding to a suggestion made under hypnosis she was obviously only half convinced. Several times during the rest of the afternoon she tried to persuade us to admit that it had been a joke and she had seen a real man. She said there was nothing 'ghostly' about him; he looked quite solid and normal.

Post-hypnotic suggestion as an explanation for Jesus' resurrection appearances does not, however, account for the one apparent 'fact' of the resurrection story, the emptiness of Jesus' tomb and the evident inability of anyone to produce the body. Yet it seems that even these elements of the story cannot be relied upon. As Professor Dieter Georgi of Harvard University has pointed out, Paul's writings omit any mention of an empty tomb, which raises the possibility that the body was still inside. Georgi suggests that the tomb was used as a place of worship, as practised to this day at the tomb of the *hasid* Hanina ben Dosa, and that the idea of the tomb being empty might well have been written into the gospel stories only after the sack of Jerusalem in 70 AD, at which time such worship would have been interrupted and the tomb perhaps actually emptied. It is a tenuous hypothesis, but then, in fairness, so is the whole gamut of theories concerning Jesus' disappearance from the tomb and subsequent 'resurrection'. Ultimately we must concede that on the basis of the available evidence, knowledge of exactly what happened is beyond us.

The one incontrovertible aspect of this matter is that the belief that Jesus had risen from the grave, whatever its origin, caught on very soon after the crucifixion and spread like wildfire. And it was embraced by an extraordinary diversity of people. The book of Acts, although biased in that, as generally agreed, it was written by the strongly pro-Gentile author responsible for the Luke gospel, is an invaluable source of information on the spread of early Christianity. One of the first believers to be mentioned in Acts is a Hellenistic Jew called Stephen. Although their ancestry and religion was Jewish, Hellenistic Jews lived in the fashionable Graeco-Roman style, and spoke the Greek language. From Josephus' information that Jesus' teaching 'attracted many Jews and many of the Greeks', Stephen's adherence need not be considered out of the ordinary. It is possible, if Dr Morton Smith's theories are valid, that Stephen received one of the special hypnotic initiations, for he is certainly spoken of as a worker of 'miracles and great signs' (Acts 6: 8). One notable feature of hypnosis is a striking change in facial expression on the part of the subject while in the 'trance' state, a phenomenon which may explain the information in Acts that, when he was before the Sanhedrin, Stephen's 'face appeared to them like the face of an angel' (Acts 6: 15). Whatever his background, like Jesus himself, Stephen chose to attack the material vanity of the Jerusalem Temple, harking back to the Isaiah text:

> With heaven my throne
> and earth my footstool
> what house could you build me
> what place could you make for my rest?
> Was not all this made by my hand?
>
> (Isaiah 66: 1, 2)

He then went on fearlessly to accuse the Jerusalem Temple authorities of having, in executing Jesus, murdered the great prophet foretold by Moses. Without in this instance even pausing to refer their prisoner to the Roman governor, those whom Stephen had attacked preremptorily stoned him to death.

Having established one Hellenist as its first hero, the book of Acts then turns to another, Saul, at whose feet Stephen's executioners are reported to have laid their clothes. Saul was a tent-maker from the Greek city of Tarsus in Asia Minor, and certainly a man who used the Greek Septuagint rather than the Hebrew scriptures. He is described as making it his mission to hunt out and arrest on behalf of the Sadducean authorities those fellow-Hellenists who had become Jesus' followers. In one of the best-known episodes in the New Testament, the book of Acts describes him, at the very height of his persecutions, being dramatically stopped in his tracks on the Damascus road, suffering a spell of blindness for three days, and having his sight returned by a disciple of Jesus called Ananias. Saul was promptly baptized, and subsequently took the name Paul. Striking a now familiar chord, Acts tells us that during his blindness Paul was dazzled by a heavenly light, heard Jesus speaking, and had a vision of him so intense that in his own writings Paul could refer to it only obliquely:

I know a man in Christ [i.e. Paul himself] who, fourteen years ago, was caught up whether still in the body or out of the body, I do not know, God knows – right into the third heaven. I do know, however, that this same person . . . was caught up into paradise and heard things which must not and cannot be put into human language. (2 Corinthians 12: 1-4)

There is a strong hint here of a hypnotic 'trip' to the kingdom of God, not least in the three days of blindness, reminiscent of the similar period the secret gospel's rich young man spent in the tomb. But quite aside from this, Paul's reference to the event clearly indicates that he had been turned in his tracks by something of considerable hypnotic force, a conversion experience regarded by modern psychiatrists such as Dr William Sargant as both psychologically convincing and a classic of its kind.

The irony in this extraordinary coup for Jesus' earliest followers lies in the character of the individual they had brought into their camp. Any other recruit to a new religion might have been expected to take time to study thoroughly the man behind the experience that had so dramatically changed his life, to learn, for example, what Jesus had taught, and some background details of his life. But Paul seems to have wanted none of this. Even the strongly pro-Pauline Acts remarks that it was 'only a few days' before Paul began actively evangelizing for Jesus, and according to Paul himself the process was even more swift:

I did not stop to discuss this with any human being, nor did I go up to Jerusalem to see those who were already apostles before me, but I went off to Arabia at once, and later went straight back from there to Damascus. Even when after three years I went to Jerusalem to visit Cephas [Peter] and stayed with him for fifteen days, I did not see any of the other apostles . . . (Galatians 1: 16-19)

As might be expected, therefore, Paul had little interest in Jesus' crucifixion as an actual and recent event, associated with flesh-and-blood individuals such as Pontius Pilate and the Jewish high priests. For him the experience of the resurrected Jesus was all he needed: '. . . the Good news I preached is not a human message that I was given by men, it is something I learned only through a revelation of Jesus Christ.'

Thus Paul saw Jesus' death on an other-worldly level, one of faith and the imagination. It was a divine plan thought out 'before the aeons', whereby the 'powers that rule the world' crucified in ignorance a supernatural 'Lord of glory' (1 Corinthians 2: 8). Instead of referring to Jesus as 'the Christ', which would have been the correct translation of 'Messiah' into Greek, Paul adopted the fashion (he most likely initiated it) of calling Jesus 'Christ' as if this was a proper name, ignoring its political connotations, and also referred to him as *the* Son of God (Acts 9: 20). And on the strength of his profound conversion experience, and being himself merely a Hellenistic Jew, he apparently decided that it should be perfectly permissible for Gentile converts to Jesus' teaching to discard traditional requirements of the Jewish Law, such as circumcision and prohibition of the eating of 'unclean' meats – requirements that during the Maccabean revolt Jews had laid down their lives to defend.

As few of today's Christians are aware, the self-styled 'apostle' Paul was not, despite his conversion, necessarily the universally revered figure within the earliest Church that is popularly supposed. This rather revolutionary idea was first proposed by the great Tübingen theologian Ferdinand Christian Baur in the nineteenth century, and has more recently been developed by Professor S.G.F. Brandon and writers such as Hugh J. Schonfield. In fact it is obvious to anyone who reads Paul's letters not as religious documents but for their historical content that it must be true. In his letter to those whom he had converted in Galatia not long before, Paul remarks on certain others who had been there after him with 'a different version of the Good News' (Galatians 1: 6). In his letter to the Corinthians he notes regretfully:

... there are serious differences among you. What I mean are all these slogans that you have, like 'I am for Paul', 'I am for Cephas [Peter]', 'I am for Christ'. (I Corinthians 1: 12–13)

Paul studiously omits to mention who his mysterious opponents are, but happens to let slip, in a typically exasperated remark in his second letter to the Corinthians, 'As far as I can tell, these arch apostles have nothing more than I have' (2 Corinthians 11: 5).

Arch apostles? Who did he mean? As modern scholars now agree, it can be deduced from the well organized nature of Paul's opponents, their close marking of his activities and his obvious embarrassed reluctance to name them, that the 'arch apostles' can have been none other than the original Jewish followers of Jesus based, during Paul's lifetime, in Jerusalem. It is rarely appreciated how little the surviving documentation tells us of the activities of Jesus' Jewish disciples after the crucifixion, but Acts does give us the occasional important though tantalizing glimpse:

The many miracles and signs worked through the apostles made a deep impression on everyone. The faithful all lived together and owned everything in common; they sold their goods and possessions and shared out the proceeds among themselves according to what each one needed. They went as a body to the Temple every day but met in their houses for the breaking of bread; they shared their food gladly and generously; they praised God and were looked up to by everyone. (Acts 2: 43–7)

In this brief description we have a picture of a group carrying out Jesus' teachings to the letter, and continuing to worship in the tradition of the old Jewish religion, just as Jesus himself had done.

Above The apostle Peter, from a third-century fresco in the Hypogeum of the Aurelii, Rome. According to the second chapter of the book of Acts, Peter was one of several who claimed to have seen Jesus alive within days of having been laid in the grave.

Above right Jesus between Peter and Paul, from a fresco in the catacomb of Ss Peter and Marcellinus, Rome. Internal politics among the early Christians led to Paul posthumously being given equal status with Jesus' disciple Peter. Letters were even forged to give an appearance of amity between Peter and Paul, although the two would appear to have been at odds during their lifetimes. As part of this process James, brother of Jesus and first head of the Jerusalem followers of Jesus, was cast into obscurity.

Right The self-styled apostle Paul, from a fourth-century diptych in the Museo Nazionale, Florence. Paul's dramatic conversion seems to have given him the confidence to work 'miracles', exemplified by his immunity from snake bite (centre panel, after Acts 28: 2–6), and his healing of the sick (lower panel). But his claims of visionary experiences caused friction among those who had known the human Jesus.

147

Strangely, what we are *not* told is anything about this group's leadership. Acts makes it clear that there was a major controversy over whether uncircumcized Gentiles should receive baptism. Jesus' disciple Peter is represented as sympathetic to a Roman centurion's eagerness to follow Jesus, and is said to have had a dream in which he apparently gave divine sanction to the eating of 'unclean' foods. From Acts we also learn that Peter expounded this revelation at a council meeting in Jerusalem, that Paul became apostle to the uncircumcised, and that an individual called James (who uses the words 'I rule ...') apparently agreed to less strictly orthodox rules being applied to pagan converts. But there is an uncomfortable suggestion here that all is not being told quite straight, an impression which gains greater cogency from an important independent, first-hand source, Paul's letter to the Galatians. In this Paul speaks of Peter initially eating with, and therefore expressing sympathy towards, uncircumcized Gentiles, but then receiving a visit from 'certain friends of James' who ask him to abandon his pro-Gentile stance, which he dutifully agrees to 'for fear of the group that insisted on circumcision' (Galatians 2: 12). Incensed at Peter's shameful volte-face, Paul tells us: 'When Cephas [Peter] came to Antioch ... I opposed him to his face, since he was manifestly in the wrong' (Galatians 2: 11).

The fascinating question here is the identity of the mysterious James, who could command the authority to overrule even Peter on such matters. Why should the book of Acts be so reticent about him? Despite the popular supposition that Peter was first head of the Church, it is clear from a variety of sources that the neglected James was its first true leader. This is explicit in the Nag Hammadi gospel of Thomas, which in Logion 12 represents Jesus naming 'James the Righteous' as the disciples' leader after his own departure. It is equally explicit in the writings of the second-century Jewish author Hegesippus and the fourth-century Eusebius of Caesarea. The latter, who quotes from Hegesippus, unequivocally speaks of James the Righteous as 'first to be elected to the episcopal throne of the Jerusalem Church'.

The most astonishing information of all, however, particularly for those Christians taught to believe that Jesus was the only son of the 'ever-virgin' Mary, is that this James was none other than Jesus' brother. This is attested by Josephus who, describing with genuine sadness James' unjust execution at the hands of a Sadducean high priest in 62 AD, refers to him as 'the brother of Jesus called the Christ'. This is corroborated by Paul, remarking of a trip to Jerusalem, 'I only saw James, the brother of the Lord' (Galatians 1: 20). It is also corroborated in the writings of Hegesippus and Eusebius. And in fact, the same information is to be found in the gospels, in a passage in which the people of Nazareth say of Jesus:

This is the carpenter, surely, the son of Mary, the brother of James and Joset and Jude and Simon? His sisters too, are they not with us? (Mark 6: 3)

Although there are frequent attempts to dismiss the significance of this passage on the grounds that 'brothers' can mean 'cousins' among Near Eastern peoples, there is every reason for believing that in this context 'brothers' and 'sisters' mean precisely that.

So why was there so great a reluctance to acknowledge James? We seem to be faced with a straight, first-century clash of theologies, Paul's on the one hand, James' on the other, and despite the authority which should be due to the latter, Paul's is all that has been allowed to come down to us. Or, in fairness, almost all.

One of the most neglected of New Testament documents is in fact a letter written by James. Dismissed by Martin Luther as 'a right strawy epistle', and tossed aside by the nineteenth-century German theologians as a work of the late second century, in his *Redating the New Testament* Dr. John Robinson has very cogently argued that it is original to James, the brother of Jesus. The letter exhibits a close similarity to Jesus' Sermon on the Mount teachings, and it reveals its early composition by portraying Jesus' followers still worshipping within the Jewish religion, but its most marked feature is its gentle but firm stance on the importance of Jesus' teaching on communal living, as distinct from Paul's stress on a Christ of faith. In James' words:

Take the case, my brothers, of someone who has never done a single good act, but claims he has faith. Will that faith save him? If one of the brothers or one of the sisters is in need of clothes and has not enough food to live on, and one of you says to them: 'I wish you well; keep yourself warm and eat plenty' without giving them these bare necessities of life, then what good is that? Faith is like that: if good works do not go with it, it is quite dead. (James 2: 14–17)

Of the fate of James, we learn from Josephus, Eusebius and Hegesippus that after leading a life of great piety, worshipping daily in the Temple, and winning great respect from the ordinary people, in 62 AD he was murdered at the instigation of one of that same Sadducee sect responsible for the death of Stephen, and of his brother Jesus. He was subsequently succeeded by Simeon, son of his uncle Cleopas, and by thirteen other 'Bishops' of Jerusalem until this line was extinguished during the Second Jewish Revolt of

132 AD. Like James and Simeon, several other 'bishops of the circumcision' appear to have been blood relatives of Jesus, indicating that, as in the case of the Zealots, leadership of Jesus' church was originally on dynastic, or 'family business' lines.

It is clear then that the years immediately following Jesus' crucifixion were not characterized by the harmony between believers that is sometimes supposed, but rather by intense rivalry between two major factions: that of James and his fellow Palestinian-born Jews, believing in Jesus and his teachings but upholding traditional observances such as circumcision, and that of Paul, his fellow Hellenists and Gentiles, likewise believing in Jesus, but maintaining that this faith, with all its hypnotic force, overrode the old requirements of the Jewish Law.

It might be thought that Paul was a particularly extreme example of the latter view, but this was in fact far from being the case. An underrated and still little understood phenomenon of the early Christian world was the meteoric growth of what may loosely be termed Gnosticism, a bewildering variety of fringe groups all believing that the personal experience of Jesus, through whatever form of spiritual inspiration, eclipsed all other considerations. One branch, the Docetists (pronounced Do-see-tists) conceived of Jesus as such a heavenly being that he could never have existed as mortal flesh and blood, but must merely have appeared human. The Montanists practised glossolalia or 'speaking with tongues', a phenomenon that still exists among such charismatic groups as the Pentecostalists. In some groups, such as the Marcionites, Jesus' emancipated view of women was given special emphasis, women being appointed as priests and bishops, causing one more orthodox churchman to complain: '... how audacious they are! They have no modesty. They are bold enough to teach, to engage in argument, to enact exorcisms, to undertake cures.' Jesus' predilection for food, wine and women was the inspiration for another group, the Carpocratians, who, according to their enemies, contended that every mortal sin needed to be experienced in order for the soul to reach heaven. The Carpocratians, among others, taught that Jesus was of normal human parentage. But the common denominator in all these groups was their freedom, their lack of formal rules and guidelines, their reliance on inspiration rather than creeds and hierarchies, and not least their avowal that they possessed some secret 'knowledge' or wisdom, hence the name 'Gnostic'. There must, it seems, have been some secret element in Jesus' original teaching that was common to all these groups and at the same time responsible for their astonishing diversity and vitality. Given the variety of human responses to hypnosis, making it to this day one of the

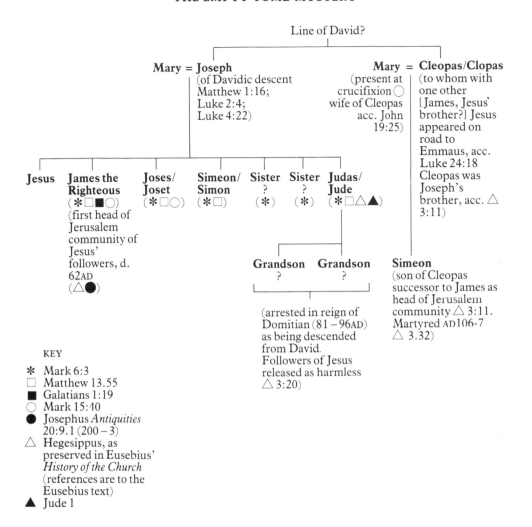

Line of David?

Mary = Joseph
(of Davidic descent
Matthew 1:16;
Luke 2:4;
Luke 4:22)

Mary = Cleopas/Clopas
(present at
crucifixion ○
wife of Cleopas
acc. John
19:25)

(to whom with
one other
[James, Jesus'
brother?] Jesus
appeared on
road to
Emmaus, acc.
Luke 24:18
Cleopas was
Joseph's
brother, acc. △
3:11)

Jesus James the Righteous (✱□■○) (first head of Jerusalem community of Jesus' followers, d. 62AD (△●) Joses/Joset (✱□○) Simeon/Simon (✱□) Sister ? (✱) Sister ? (✱) Judas/Jude (✱□△▲)

Grandson ? Grandson ?

(arrested in reign of Domitian (81 – 96AD) as being descended from David. Followers of Jesus released as harmless △ 3:20)

Simeon
(son of Cleopas
successor to James as
head of Jerusalem
community △ 3:11.
Martyred AD106-7
△ 3.32)

KEY
✱ Mark 6:3
□ Matthew 13.55
■ Galatians 1:19
○ Mark 15:40
● Josephus *Antiquities*
   20:9.1 (200 – 3)
△ Hegesippus, as
   preserved in Eusebius'
   History of the Church
   (references are to the
   Eusebius text)
▲ Jude 1

Family tree of Jesus, based on assumption that the 'brothers and sisters' listed in Mark 6: 3, and mentioned elsewhere (John 7: 2; Acts 1: 14; 1 Corinthians 9: 5), were Jesus' immediate family. This is certainly how they were regarded by early authorities such as Tertullian and Hegesippus. Note how headship of the Jerusalem followers of Jesus passed to members of Jesus' family, his brother James, then his cousin Simeon. A similar family tradition is to be noted among leadership of the Zealots. According to Harvard University's Professor Helmut Koester the Judas or Jude mentioned in canonical sources as a brother of Jesus may be identified with the Didymus Judas Thomas – Judas 'the twin' (brother of Jesus?) – whom the Nag Hammadi 'Gospel of Thomas' represents as its author. Although there is some support for this idea within the traditions of the Syrian church, the 'Thomas' author, if he was genuinely apostolic, may be better identified with the disciple of that name.

most unpredictable of phenomena, is it possible that this was the mystery element?

Somehow, from these myriad groups of early followers of Jesus – Jewish Christians, Pauline Christians, Gnostic Christians – there evolved the canonical New Testament and the various forms of Christianity that we identify with today. The explanation for this seems to lie in certain accidents of history. By the 60s AD adherence to Jesus' teachings among both Jews and Gentiles had already spread widely, if inevitably thinly, across the Roman Empire and beyond. When Paul, at the beginning of the decade, arrived in Rome there was already a community of 'brothers' to greet him (Acts 28: 15), and a strong patristic tradition attests to Peter's presence in the city at roughly the same time. But terrible troubles were in store. Within six years of the death of James the Righteous in 62 AD, it appears that both Peter and Paul were executed in Rome, during the period when the Emperor Nero was using Christians as scapegoats for the city's disastrous fire. In 66 AD, in Jesus' homeland, there began the four bloody years of the Jewish revolt, which caused terrible loss of life, the desolation of Jerusalem, and the total destruction of the Temple, and culminated in the noble but tragic suicide of the defenders of Masada in 74 AD. Although some semblance of a Jewish Christian bishopric seems to have survived until the Bar Kokhba revolt of 132 AD, essentially the loss of the Temple, even though the Sadducees and their corruption were also wiped out, marked the breaking point with Judaism for at least some of Jesus' followers. There could no longer be any strong justification for Jerusalem remaining the new movement's spiritual headquarters.

It seems to have been this eventuality, coupled with an intense wave of anti-Jewish feeling across the Empire, which provided the opportunity to free Jesus' teaching from the Jewish Law so craved for by the pro-Pauline faction. With the 'circumcision' party in disarray, decimated and scattered like all other Palestinian Jews, the gospel of Jesus could now be written and promulgated unconstrainedly from a Gentile standpoint. For those converts living in Graeco–Roman cities it was expedient to play down Jesus' association with the Jewish people and with Messianism, and also to deflect attention from the Jewish party represented by James. Even Jesus' resurrection appearance to James, mentioned by Paul and independently attested in a preserved portion of the otherwise lost gospel according to the Hebrews, goes unmentioned by the canonical gospel writers, although James was almost certainly the unnamed companion of his uncle Cleopas, referred to in Luke's account of Jesus' appearance on the road to Emmaus (Luke 24: 13–32).

Above Masada. Here in 74 AD 960 Jewish men, women and children chose collective suicide rather than surrender to the besieging Romans. Although there was a brief period of resistance during the Bar-Kokhba revolt (132-5 AD), Jewish confidence had been shattered, and surviving religious leaders took their stand on traditional Pharisaism rather than the innovative teachings of Jesus. The future for what we now call 'Christianity' lay in the Gentile world.

Right Fragment of Greek inscription prohibiting Gentiles from entering the inner areas of the Jerusalem Temple on pain of death. Discovered in 1935, this tablet is now in the Rockefeller Museum, Jerusalem. According to Josephus there were similar notices in Latin. Scuffles associated with this prohibition led to Paul's arrest by the Romans, initially for his own safety, as he claimed his rights as a Roman citizen.

There was a correspondingly strong incentive to represent Jesus as sympathetic to Gentiles, hence Luke's and Matthew's stories of his cure of a centurion's servant (Matthew 8: 5–13; Luke 7: 1–10), even though we are told elsewhere that he avowed 'I was sent only to the lost sheep of the House of Israel' (Matthew 15: 24).

Inevitably the process of imposing on the new religion a Gentile bias was a complex one, and was influenced by the individual character of the Jewish and other communities in the centres where the canonical gospels are thought to have been composed. But it was at this point that the gospels as we know them today were probably written, Paul's letters preserved for posterity as sacred literature, and some literary adulteration indulged in to paper over the still gaping cracks between Jewish and Gentile outlooks. To cite examples of such tampering, modern theological studies suggest that the New Testament's two letters of Peter, the second speaking unctuously and unconvincingly of 'our brother Paul ... so dear to us' (2 Peter 3: 15), were most likely forged in Peter's name by some pro-Pauline writer, and that other letters attributed to Paul, notably the Pastorals, were fabricated to create a false impression of harmony. Recent computer tests have clearly confirmed what theological scholars have long suspected, that whoever wrote Paul's letters to Timothy and Titus was not the person (indisputably Paul) who wrote Galatians, Romans and Corinthians.

Thus was born what can now, for the first time, legitimately be labelled 'Christianity' as a distinct religion in its own right, rather than a mere branch of the old Jewish religion – though the original Jesus almost certainly intended that it should be nothing more than Judaism with a new slant. It was an extraordinary, tangled birth for a religious movement that has so successfully captured millions of hearts and minds.

Sadly, because of inadequate and one-sided documentation, very little of the circumstances surrounding its birth are yet understood. We know almost nothing, for example, of the fate of those followers of Jesus who remained faithful to the Jewish Law, variously labelled 'Nazarenes' and 'Jewish Christians'. One tradition associates them with settling at Pella on the east coast of the Jordan. Another suggests that they may have been one and the same as the 'Ebionites' or 'Poor Ones' condemned as heretics by the fourth-century Bishop Epiphanius. According to Epiphanius, although the Ebionites recognized Jesus as Messiah and followed his teachings, they, like the Carpocratians, regarded him as of normal human parentage, and they followed the old Jewish Law. They had their own Jewish language gospel, which may have been the 'sayings' collected by Matthew, together with their own book of 'Acts' (quite different from the Lukan one) and an 'Ascents of James'. Perhaps not surprisingly, they deprecated the writings of Paul, dismissing him as no true Jew. Also lost to us are anything more than snippets of information on the different Gnostic groups, most of their writings, with the exception of the Nag Hammadi hoard, having similarly disappeared.

The lack of such documentation is often attributed to the centuries of persecution suffered by the multifarious sects of early Christians, persecutions which could be savage and barbaric under Emperors such as Nero (54–68 AD), Domitian (81–96 AD), and Decius (249–51 AD). But equally, under civilized Emperors such as Hadrian (117–138 AD) and Antoninus Pius (138–161 AD), there were long periods of unofficial toleration. While, under Hadrian, the Jews suffered appalling losses during the Bar Kokhba revolt, with only the Pharisaic group surviving to lay the groundwork of modern Judaism, in Rome the Christians enjoyed sufficient toleration to organize their religion under presbyters, bishops and deacons, and even to build a proper shrine over the earth grave in which Jesus' disciple Peter was believed to have been laid. Recently rediscovered, this shrine has been found to have originally formed part of a walled structure that may have been the world's earliest church building, complete with a courtyard for the congregation, and in one corner a tiny room with a low doorway. Inside this room were found the remains of an old cistern. Was this a baptistry where something along the lines of Morton Smith's secret rite, although fast becoming forgotten, was still being performed? The design is by no means incompatible with the idea.

The intermittent outbreaks of persecution were not necessarily responsible, therefore, for the loss of early Christian documentation, and to find the real cause of its disappearance we must turn to the Roman political scene in the opening years of the fourth century AD. At this time the Emperor Diocletian, ruling a much divided Empire with three co-Emperors, Galerius, Constantius and Maximian, had decided to emulate Nero and Decius by instituting a particularly savage crackdown on the Empire's now substantial Christian population. He ordered Christian scriptures to be burnt, and all those failing to honour the pagan gods to be mutilated and deported. Although its like had been seen before, for all varieties of Christians it was a tragic episode. Yet, as they could scarcely have dared to hope, deliverance was close at hand.

Waiting in the wings was Constantine, son of the co-Emperor Constantius, ready to make his own mark on the Empire's history by overturning the long years of strife and disunity and granting the Christians their first truly official toleration. But as events would prove, for many groups who genuinely considered themselves to be Christian, Constantine's 'toleration' would claim its own terrible price.

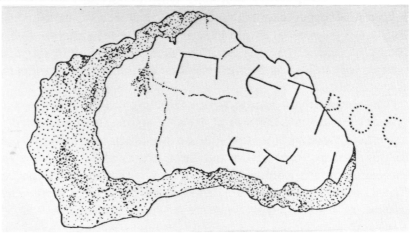

Since 1939 excavations under the high altar of St Peter's, Rome, have uncovered masonry from a shrine built during the fourth century by Constantine the Great. This shrine in its turn appears to have been built over a red-walled building, possibly Rome's earliest Christian church, featuring a mid-second century Tropaion, or shrine, which according to some interpretations marked Peter's actual grave. Subject of heated controversy is an inscription on a piece of plaster from the red wall, which seems to read, in Greek letters, 'PETR[OS] ENI', 'Peter is within'.

HOW HE BECAME GOD

BY 312 AD, only nine years since Diocletian had begun his persecution of Christians, the whole political face of the Empire had been changed. Diocletian had abdicated, Galerius was dead, Constantine's father Constantius was dead, and in the West only Maximian's son Maxentius lay between Constantine and control of the whole western half of the Roman Empire. On 28 October 312, having stormed his way through northern Italy, Constantine, tall and bull-necked, reviewed with his generals his final plans for the capture of Rome itself, just ten miles to the south.

It was no easy task. Behind Rome's walls Maxentius had the advantage of superior numbers, well prepared defences, and command of the Empire's premier fighting force, the Praetorian Guard, men whose power for centuries had determined who should be Caesar in the capital city. Nor could Constantine, as aggressor, expect much enthusiasm from Rome's citizens, already weary of the seemingly endless troubles of the last few years, and their daily existence now threatened with disruption by yet another Roman's bid for mastery over another. Constantine was badly in need of something to give his cause extra purpose and justification. As is now part of Christian legend, on the very night before the battle Constantine had a dream in which he was shown a sign, accompanied by the words: *Hoc signo victor eris*! 'By this sign you shall be the victor!' The sign consisted of the Greek letters Chi-Rho, the first two letters of the name Christ, in a monogram form that had recently been adopted by the still persecuted group called Christians, of whom, as Constantine was well aware, there were a considerable number among the ordinary citizens of Rome. That the original Christ preached a form of pacifism would almost certainly never have occurred to Constantine. For him the Chi-Rho seemed an inspired sign to fight by, and at dawn he gave orders for it to be painted on every soldier's shield.

Meanwhile, to the south, Maxentius had planned what seemed to him a brilliant piece of defensive strategy. Having prepared particularly strong

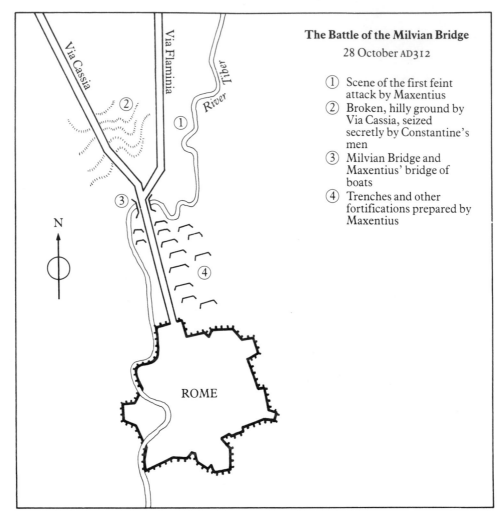

The Battle of the Milvian Bridge

28 October AD312

1. Scene of the first feint attack by Maxentius
2. Broken, hilly ground by Via Cassia, seized secretly by Constantine's men
3. Milvian Bridge and Maxentius' bridge of boats
4. Trenches and other fortifications prepared by Maxentius

fortifications south of Rome's Milvian Bridge, he wanted to persuade Constantine to attack from this direction. His plan was to make a feint northerly advance on Constantine's position, pretend to retreat by crossing a bridge of boats he had specially built alongside the Milvian Bridge, which was narrow and already four centuries old, then cut the boats loose as soon as his own troops were safely across the river. The intention was that part of Constantine's army, in hot pursuit across the boat-bridge, would be trapped on the boats, drifting helplessly downstream, while the rest, funnelled on to the narrow stone bridge, could be cut down with ease the moment they set foot off it.

The Milvian Bridge, Rome. But for a battle fought here on 28 October 312 AD Christianity might never have become the world religion we know today. Already more than four hundred years old at the time of the battle, the bridge has altered little since it was built.

The battle of the Milvian Bridge. Detail from a relief on the Arch of Constantine, Rome, showing Maxentius and his troops falling into the Tiber.

Unfortunately for Maxentius, things went badly wrong. Constantine, by an outflanking movement, threatened to cut off the carefully planned escape route. As a result, what should have been an orderly manoeuvre by Maxentius' troops was instead a mad scramble for the boat-bridge. In the confusion the boats were cut loose too soon by Maxentius' engineers. Some of the defending army found themselves cast adrift, while many others were trapped between Constantine's army and the Tiber; their only exit, the Milvian Bridge, was inevitably too narrow for their numbers, and hundreds simply fell or hurled themselves into the water in full armour. In this way Maxentius himself died, and his corpse was soon afterwards found washed up downstream. He was swiftly decapitated, and with this gruesome trophy dripping from a lance Constantine made his triumphal entry into Rome later that day, the Christian monogram still emblazoned on his soldiers' shields. In a fashion its founder could scarcely have anticipated, the religion of Jesus of Nazareth, or at least a semblance of it, had captured Rome.

The events of that day marked the turning point from which Christianity became the world religion we know now. Constantine was clearly grateful for his victory and made it part of his policy to set Christianity on course. Altogether more obscure, however, is the relationship between his brand of Christianity and the intentions of Jesus. Certainly Constantine does not appear to have been recognizably Christian before his victory. Only six years before the Milvian Bridge battle he had had hundreds of Frankish rebel prisoners torn to pieces in an arena. He had stood by without apparent qualm while Galerius, following up Diocletian's anti-Christian policy, had supervised the burning of Christian sacred texts and the mutilation of those who refused sacrifice to the pagan gods. Even after his victory the triumphal arch erected in his honour, which stands to this day alongside the Colosseum, was adorned with traditional pagan symbols. A commemorative medallion struck by Constantine in 313 AD portrays him as Invictus Constantinus alongside the image of Sol Invictus, the god of a pagan cult imported from Syria a few decades earlier by the Emperor Aurelian. Even eleven years after winning the battle at the Milvian Bridge Constantine murdered his already vanquished rival Licinius, former Emperor in the East; he then killed his wife, by having her boiled alive in her bath, and his own son – hardly the action of a true follower of Jesus.

Properly to understand Constantine, we need to recognize that for him politics came first, and matters of religion (or at least religious ethics as we understand them today) a very poor second. Having set himself to conquer a vast and hitherto bitterly divided Empire, his first concern had to be the

Above Commemorative medallion issued by Constantine *c.*313 AD, portraying himself alongside the pagan sun god Sol Invictus.

Above right Commemorative medallion issued by Constantine *c.*315 AD, in which a tiny Chi-Rho, as a symbol of Christianity, appears on Constantine's helmet. But the horse's head, representative of the chariot of the sun god, indicates a continuing pagan influence.

Jesus as sun god, riding in the solar chariot. Third-century mosaic from the Mausoleum of the Julii, discovered during excavations beneath the high altar of St Peter's, Rome. This is another indication of the synthesis of pagan and Christian thinking. To any original Jewish follower of Jesus such a representation would have been unthinkable.

matter of unity. Never disloyal to supporters, from the very outset of his rule in Rome he granted toleration both to Christianity and to followers of every other religion in the Empire, Mithraists, Jews, adherents to the traditional Graeco-Roman pantheon, and many others. In unequivocal recognition of the Christians, with whom he clearly identified himself, he lavished money on the erection of basilicas both in Rome and elsewhere in the Empire, and gave over an imperial palace on the Lateran Hill as a residence for Rome's bishops. Equally there could have been nothing but a shrewd desire for unity in his adoption of the Sol Invictus cult. Essentially a simple cult of the sun, followers of Orpheus, Mithras or Apollo could all find common ground in it. Nor could the Christians grumble. Although in the East there lingered an abhorrence, inspired by the Jews, for representational images, in the West Christians had begun representing Jesus in the guise of the sun god Apollo or Orpheus, the priest of the sun. A third-century mosaic from the Mausoleum of the Julii underneath present-day St Peter's in Rome actually portrays Jesus as Sol Invictus, driving the horses of the sun's chariot. That Constantine himself mixed Christianity and the Sol Invictus cult is clear from a second commemorative medallion issued by him within two years of the first, on which he represented himself with a Chi-Rho monogram on his helmet, and with a leaping Sol chariot horse below. How far Jesus had become divorced in western Christians' minds from the Jew of history is forcefully illustrated by a portrait of him as a beardless Apollo-like youth in a mosaic that once decorated the floor of the Romano-Christian villa at Hinton St Mary in Dorset. Only the Chi-Rho monogram identifies it as Jesus. To what extent Constantine was aware of all the contradictions it is impossible to tell, but there are at least some signs that he recognized the incompatibility between Jesus' teachings and the demands of governing the Roman Empire. It was only when he was approaching death that he asked for, or was accepted for, Christian baptism. As was still the custom, he received this naked, thereafter renouncing forever the purple of his imperial rank.

If Christianity had an unorthodox champion in Constantine, he for his part acquired an extraordinary assortment of subjects in those who called themselves Christians in his time. There were bitter divisions between the *traditores*, or traitors, who had betrayed their fellow Christians, surrendered Christian books and offered pagan sacrifices during the recent Roman persecutions, and those who had suffered mutilation and hard labour rather than do so. There were equally deep divisions between Christians from Rome and those from Alexandria and from Antioch. In Alexandria, Doce-

Portrait of Jesus, from fourth-century Roman
mosaic discovered in 1963 at Hinton St Mary,
Dorset. Only the Chi-Rho monogram identifies
the portrait as Jesus; otherwise it has clearly
been influenced by representations of the pagan
god Apollo. This is one of several examples of
how, by the time of Constantine the Great, the
concept of Jesus was far removed from that of a
human Galilean Jew.

163

tism, the concept that Jesus had existed as a spirit rather than a human, had theoretically been stamped out. Nonetheless there persisted the belief that Jesus must have been too much of a god, *the* God, to have had normal bodily needs such as eating, drinking and excretion. As Clement of Alexandria, the bishop responsible for the 'secret gospel' letter, had written in the second century:

> It would be ridiculous to imagine that the body of the Redeemer, in order to exist, had the usual needs of man. He only took food and ate it in order that we should not teach about him in a Docetic fashion.

In Constantine's time the Alexandrian Archdeacon Athanasius, later to become the city's bishop, took essentially the same view: 'The Word disguised himself by appearing in a body ... by the works he did in the body [he] showed himself to be, not man, but God'. According to the Alexandrians, therefore, Jesus had been God, and had existed in total equality with God since before time began. To view him any other way made him less than God, which was unthinkable.

However, for those who had grown up around Antioch, the region that included the homeland of the earthly Jesus, there was an altogether different emphasis and outlook. In the third century the great Lucian of Antioch, reflecting Christianity's origins in Jewish monotheism, had stressed the essential oneness of God, the simple humanity of Jesus, and the importance of the way of life Jesus taught, which those obsessed with theology too easily overlooked. One of those who had been taught by Lucian was a magnetic, ascetic-looking priest and preacher called Arius, who went on to officiate within the Alexandrian diocese. Here he attracted a substantial following, especially among women, and popularized the Lucianic view with a book of 'Happy Thoughts', some of which he set into the form of simple songs:

> God was not always Father
> Once he was not the Father
> Afterwards he became the Father.

Inevitably such views invoked the hostility of Alexandria's Bishop Alexander, supreme ecclesiastical authority for the Egyptian and Libyan region. Arius found himself excommunicated, and not unexpectedly sought support from leading churchmen whom he knew to hold views similar to his own, men such as the powerful Bishops Eusebius of Caesarea and Eusebius of Nicomedia, both former Lucian pupils. Eusebius of Nicomedia did not let his colleague down. He immediately summoned a synod of the bishops in his region, formally supporting Arius and condemning the Alexandrian viewpoint.

Constantine, who had just won the eastern half of the Empire, thereby at last achieving his cherished goal of unity, suddenly found himself in the midst of this seething dispute between two rival groups of Christians, with epithets such as 'maniacs', 'eels', 'cuttlefish', 'atheists' and 'wolves' being hurled between one faction and the other. The extent to which Constantine, of no great education, even understood the theological issues is by no means clear, but he tried to pacify the protagonists by sending an identical letter to both Arius and Alexander, almost unctuously pleading for 'equal forbearance' and reconciliation:

Constantine the Victor, Supreme Augustus, to Alexander and Arius . . . how deep a wound has not only my ears but my heart received from the report that divisions exist among yourselves . . . having enquired carefully into the origin and foundation of these differences, I find their cause to be of a truly insignificant nature, quite unworthy of such bitter contention . . . Restore my quiet days and untroubled nights to me, so that joy of undimmed light, delight in a tranquil life, may once again be mine.

Unfortunately, from a distance even Constantine was unable to smooth such troubled waters. Nor was there any supreme ecclesiastical authority to whom the matter could be referred. No one 'Pope' as such existed, the Bishops of Rome, Alexandria and Antioch each being recognized as having supreme authority within their respective geographical regions, but no supremacy over all Christendom. Accordingly, to resolve this and other issues (such as the date of Easter, another bitter source of contention), Constantine decided personally to summon all Christian leaders to the first-ever 'World Council'. The appointed date was early summer 325 AD, the venue the pleasant lakeside town of Nicaea, today Iznik in north-western Turkey, where Constantine had a suitably commodious palace.

From the very circumstances of the time, it was bound to be an extraordinary gathering. With Christianity having spread as far as Britain in the West and India in the East, for some of the delegates the journey took several weeks, if not months. When they assembled, it was to set eyes on each other for the first time in many cases, though for several, such as Bishop Pamphnutius, sight was denied because they had been viciously blinded during earlier persecutions. The hermit Jacob of Nisibis arrived in goatskins, accompanied by a persistent horde of gnats. Another delegate was the saintly Nicholas from the city of Myra in Asia Minor, who was the prototype of the

Christmas Santa Claus. Also present of course was Arius. Although the Bishop of Rome excused himself as too old to travel, he sent two priests to represent him. Before this bizarre and unprecedented assembly Constantine, dazzlingly robed and dripping with gold and jewels of a decadence earlier Emperors would have abhorred, took his place on a low, wrought gold chair.

It was at this point in history, and before this assembly, that a decision was to be made that would have the most profound consequences for believers in Jesus Christ to this day. In the simplest of terms, the point at issue was whether Jesus was a mere being (now incontestably divine) who had been brought into existence to serve God's purpose – to act as the 'word' of God – at a particular time in the early first century AD, or whether he had been God for all eternity, 'of one substance with the Father' (as those in the West expressed it). If the latter, then he was effectively a supraterrestrial entity easily compatible with Sol Invictus, but light years removed from the Jesus envisaged by Arius and the Antiochenes.

Although reports of the exact proceedings of the Council of Nicaea have not survived, from those contemporary accounts that do exist it would seem that Eusebius of Nicomedia and Eusebius of Caesarea, representing the Antiochene party, forcefully espoused the Arian view, confidently expecting that they would win the day. To try to provide a formula on which the whole gathering could agree, Eusebius of Caesarea read out the statement of belief which he was accustomed to employ at baptisms within his own diocese:

We believe in one God, the Father, the Almighty, maker of all that is seen and unseen; and in one lord Jesus Christ, the word of God, god from God, light from light, life from life, only begotten son, first-born of all creation, before all ages begotten from the Father, who for our salvation was incarnate and lived among men . . .

It is important to recognize that while the distinctions implied by capital letters today did not exist in Constantine's time (as mentioned earlier, only uncials were employed then) as set out above they convey what Eusebius and the other Antiochenes essentially intended. To most Catholics the words will have a familiar ring because at every Mass they recite almost the same formula. For many present-day Christians the words more than adequately impart a divinity to Jesus, particularly in quite illogically accrediting him 'first-born of all creation'. But to the fourth-century Alexandrians, as was made clear by the brilliantly eloquent Archdeacon Athanasius (acting as spokesman for his aged bishop, Alexander), it simply did not go far enough, and was not sufficiently precise. It made Jesus appear less than God himself.

Colossal head of Constantine
the great, from the Palace of
the Curators, Rome. In giving
Christianity official status,
Constantine secured its
future, but in the process he
radically altered the
founder's original
intentions.

For the judgment of Solomon on the issue, the only appropriate recourse was to Constantine, almost certainly theologically illiterate, but politically a superb man manager. Exactly what swayed Constantine in that crucial moment we shall probably never know. There can be little doubt that for him the deification of a man was nothing particularly special. He had had his father Constantius deified, would be accorded the same honour after his own death, and would surely have expected Jesus to be a superior entity in the divine hierarchy. He might well also have taken into account Alexandria's strategic and commercial advantages. Whatever his motives, Constantine ruled in favour of the Alexandrians, Eusebius' formula was heavily edited to accommodate the Alexandrian view, and, while affirming that the standpoint of the Antiochenes was entirely reasonable, Constantine urged all Council delegates to sign the revised formula as a statement of faith on which all Christians should in future agree. For all those who signed, there was the inducement of an invitation to stay on at Nicaea as Constantine's guests for his twentieth anniversary celebrations. For those who refused there was immediate banishment. Among all concerned, it appears to have gone entirely unnoticed that the formula they were about to impose on all Christians contained not one jot of the ethical teachings that the human Jesus had once preached. Perhaps not unexpectedly, all but two of the most die-hard Arian loyalists signed. But from the none too truthful face-saving letter Eusebius of Caesarea sent back to his home diocese, it is clear how uneasy he felt about the extent to which he had compromised the fundamental principles of what he had been taught about Jesus. Other signatories, who were equally swayed into aquiescence by their awe of the forceful Constantine, felt exactly the same. Only on returning home did Eusebius of Nicomedia, Maris of Chalcedon and Theognis of Nicaea summon the courage to express to Constantine in writing how much they regretted having put their signatures to the Nicene formula: 'We committed an impious act, O Prince', wrote Eusebius of Nicomedia, 'by subscribing to a blasphemy from fear of you'.

But it was too late. An overwhelming majority of Christianity's highest dignitaries had put pens to parchment, and even though the Arian controversy would rumble on for another two or three centuries, effectively there was no turning back. Although no gospel regarded Jesus as God, and not even Paul had done so, the Jewish teacher had been declared *Very* God through all eternity, and a whole new theology would flow from this. A fourth-century sarcophagus preserved at San Paolo fuori le Mura in Rome ludicrously depicts the Trinity as three bearded men side by side, and a beardless Jesus officiating at the expulsion of Adam and Eve from the Garden

So-called Dogmatic Sarcophagus from San
Paolo fuori le Mura, Rome. This was probably
carved as a set-piece refutation of the ideas of
Arius. Jesus is represented beardless with
Adam and Eve, thereby suggesting he was
present at the time of Creation. Separately he,
with God the Father and God the Holy Spirit,
are depicted as three identical, bearded old
men. Such concepts are worlds away from the
original Jewish thinking concerning Jesus.

Alexandria, from a sixth-century mosaic in
the church of St John the Baptist, Jerash,
Jordan. At the time of Nicaea the port of
Alexandria was one of the Empire's greatest
cities, and had only recently been acquired by
Constantine during his wars of re-unification.
Although the Alexandrians had arguably
overstressed Jesus' divinity, it would have
been politically inopportune for Constantine
to alienate them by making an adverse
theological decision at Nicaea.

of Eden. Jesus, with his Jewish abhorrence of any representational images, would surely not have approved of this.

Merely to enumerate the many ways in which the original concepts of Jesus and his teachings were adulterated as a result of Constantine's actions and the consequences of the Council of Nicaea would take a book in itself. There can be no better example of the distortions that took place, however, than occurred in respect of the cult of Mary, mother of Jesus. In Constantine's time interest in her had been negligible and, even later in the fourth century, churchmen such as Helvidius and Jovinian pointed out the clear gospel evidence that Mary had given birth to several children after Jesus. Besides the list of Jesus' brothers and sisters in the Mark gospel (6: 3), Luke unequivocally describes Jesus as Mary's 'first-born', and the Matthew gospel, in the original Greek, speaks of her husband Joseph having no intercourse with Mary 'until her son was born', strongly suggesting that they had normal sexual relations afterwards. But at the very time Helvidius and Jovinian were making their point, others such as Hilary of Poitiers and the Alexandrian Didymus the Blind were in the process of bestowing on Mary the title 'Ever Virgin'. And, of course, with Jesus having been made Very God, it was inevitably not long before someone began to speculate on his mother's position. Sure enough, in the year 431, just a few miles down the coast from Nicaea, the proposition was put to the Council of Ephesus that Mary should henceforth be entitled *Theotokos* – God-bearing, and thereby 'Mother of God'. As at Nicaea, there was an Antiochene resistance movement, spearheaded by Nestorius, Bishop of Constantinople, who argued strongly that Mary could only be the mother of Jesus' humanity, but to no avail. Yet another Alexandrian, the famous patriarch Cyril, packed the Ephesus meeting with his own supporters before most Antiochenes could arrive, and the cult of Mary was firmly on its way. In 1854 Pope Pius IX made it an article of faith for all Catholics that Mary should be considered 'immaculately conceived' – that is, from the moment of her conception incapable of sin. A century later Pope Pius XII pronounced her 'Queen of Heaven'.

Another consequence of the Council of Nicaea concerned the Jews. Already the gulf that separated them from Christianity, which had begun as a movement faithful to Judaism, was wide, but once Jesus was declared Very God it became totally unbridgeable. For the Christian camp, however, the Nicaea decision carried with it an implication far more sinister. If Jesus was God, then the Jews had killed God. And whether or not this had been rationalized and accepted in Constantine's time, he certainly rescinded his

Mary, 'Mother of God', from a mosaic in the cathedral at Torcello, Italy. The Greek letters MPΘV are abbreviations of the Greek for 'Mother of God', a title which was accorded to Mary, most markedly in the West, from the fifth century onwards.

The cruel face of anti-semitism. Following Nicaea, Jews increasingly became identified as God-slayers in Christian eyes. In Hieronymous Bosch's 'Christ carrying his Cross', painted c.1510, each Jewish face is depicted as a loathsome caricature, except of course, that of Jesus, who does not count as a Jew. Such misguided thinking has contributed to centuries of Jewish persecution.

earlier overture of toleration towards them, and thrust them into a period of darkness, of which there were to be many more in their history. In the words of Jacob R. Marcus in *The Jews in the Mediaeval World:*

The Middle Ages, for the Jew at least, begin with the advent to power of Constantine the Great. He was the first Roman Emperor to issue laws which radically limited the rights of Jews as citizens of the Roman Empire, a right conferred on them by Caracalla in 212. As Christianity grew in power it influenced the emperors to limit further the civil and political rights of the Jews.

But if times were again difficult for the Jews, for the Christian Gnostics and other fringe groups they were impossible. The books of Arius and his sympathizers were ordered to be burnt, and a reign of terror proclaimed for all those who did not conform with the new, official 'Christian' line:

Understand now by this present statute, Novatians, Valentinians, Marcionites, Paulinians, you who are called Cataphrygians ... with what a tissue of lies and vanities, with what destructive and venomous errors, your doctrines are inextricably woven! We give you warning ... Let none of you presume, from this time forward, to meet in congregations. To prevent this, we command that you be deprived of all the houses in which you have been accustomed to meet ... and that these should be handed over immediately to the catholic [i.e. universal] church.

Within a generation, hardly leaving a trace of their existence for posterity, the great majority of these groups simply died away as successive 'Christian' Emperors reiterated the policies that Constantine had pursued. But in about 370 AD an unknown person trudged from what was probably the monastery of St Pachomius in Upper Egypt to bury the red earthenware jar that would be rediscovered as the Nag Hammadi hoard some sixteen centuries later. Without doubt this represents a mere fraction, and not necessarily a representative one, of the lost Gnostic and other material. It can scarcely have been a coincidence that with the dying out of the various fringe groups there also died much of the breathtaking dynamism that had fired the healings and exorcisms carried out since the time of Jesus himself.

A new era was ushered in. On the site of the shrine marking Peter's grave Constantine erected a giant basilica, which would assume yet more grandiose proportions at the behest of the power-seeking popes of the Late Renaissance – magnificent, of course, perhaps exceeding even Herod's Temple. But somehow, in all the jostling to make the Bishop of Rome supreme pontiff over all Churches, the words of the man at the root of it all had been almost forgotten:

You know that among the pagans their so-called rulers lord it over them, and their great men make their authority felt. This is not to happen among you. (Mark 10: 41, 42)

Equally neglected was the memory that the true first head of this church had been a humble Jerusalem Jew called James.

Overleaf The face on the negative of the Turin Shroud. Whether this is a genuine grave-cloth imprint or the work of an imaginative artist, no other portrayal so subtly conveys the enigma of Jesus. Did this man really rise from the dead?

THE REAL JESUS

IN the light of all the evidence discussed so far there is one question which anyone, whatever his religious persuasion, may feel impelled to ask. Would the Jew who walked the byways of Galilee in the first century AD have endorsed the Nicene Creed formulated in his name three hundred years later? The question might appear to be theological, but it should also be possible to find the historical answer.

To do so it is necessary to take ourselves back to the times in which Christianity came into being. It is fundamentally important to appreciate how easy it was, in the Gentile world at least, for an ordinary man to be believed to be a god. At least as early as the reign of Tiberius, who was Jesus' contemporary, Roman Emperors worked hard to cultivate a divine image, just as kings and pharaohs had done for centuries before them. It was commonplace for artists and sculptors to be commissioned to portray the Emperor as Zeus/Jupiter or Heracles, and the Emperor's image on legionary standards was an object of worship for the army. When Tiberius' nephew Germanicus died, a beautiful cameo was made of the youth being received into the heavenly pantheon, with the former Emperor Augustus among the gods. That such deification could be accorded to living men is evident from the account in Acts of Paul and Barnabas healing a cripple in the Asia Minor town of Lystra, in Lycaonia:

A man sat there (in Lystra) who had never walked in his life, because his feet were crippled from birth; and as he listened to Paul preaching, he managed to catch his eye. Seeing that the man had the faith to be cured, Paul said in a loud voice, 'Get to your feet – stand up' and the cripple jumped up and began to walk. When the crowd saw what Paul had done they shouted in the language of Lycaonia 'These people are gods who have come down to us disguised as men.' They addressed Barnabas as Zeus, and since Paul was the principal speaker, they called him Hermes. The priests of Zeus-outside-the-Gate, proposing that all the people should offer sacrifice with them, brought garlanded oxen to the gates. When the apostles Barnabas and Paul heard what was happening, they tore their clothes and rushed into the crowd, shouting 'Friends, what do you think you are doing? We are only human beings like you . . .' Even this speech, however, was scarcely enough to stop the crowd offering them sacrifice. (Acts 14: 8–18)

Even the Jewish world, permeated as it was with Hellenism, was susceptible to such ideas. The story is told of Herod the Great's grandson, Herod Agrippa, who in the decade that Jesus was crucified was thrown into prison for suspected treachery against Tiberius. On his first day of captivity an owl was seen to alight on a branch above Agrippa's head, and an old German prisoner, noticing this, told him it was a good omen: he would shortly be released and regain his royal status. But the German also warned that when Agrippa saw the bird again, he would die within five days. Just as predicted, Agrippa was released, and in 37 AD became King of the Jews, ruling over Herod the Great's former territories. At the height of his power, in 44 AD he attended in great style the quadrennial Roman games at Caesarea, appearing in dazzling robes of silver, which sparkled in the sunshine. Sycophants around him cried out that he was a god not a man, and Agrippa, flattered, failed to reprove them. It was his fatal mistake. He looked up . . . and there was the owl, flying towards him. Seized by sudden stomach pains, he died in agony five days later, 'eaten away with worms', as noted with relish in Acts 12: 23. Whether or not this is just a good story, it is the clearest possible example of how easily pagans would acclaim a man as a god. It also clearly conveys what a fatal blasphemy it was for a Jew even to think in these terms.

From all that we know of Jesus, is it possible that he regarded himself as God? The gospels' answer is clear. In the Mark gospel, the most consistent in conveying Jesus' humanity, a man is represented as running up to Jesus and addressing him with the words 'Good master'. Jesus' response is a firm rebuke: 'Why do you call me good? No one is good but God alone' (Mark 10: 18). Even in the John gospel, the one most inclined to make Jesus divine, he is reported as stating quite categorically, 'the Father is greater than I' (John 14: 28), which should have been enough to spike the Alexandrian guns at Nicaea.

If Jesus had wanted to institute a formula for the religion he taught, there is one moment, described in Mark's gospel, when he had the perfect opportunity to do so. A scribe is reported as having asked him: 'Which is the first of all the commandments?' It was an occasion to which Jesus could have imparted one of his characteristic twists, bringing in something new, something involving himself, if he wished us to believe that he was a member of a Trinity, on an equal footing with God the Father. Instead he unhesitatingly looked to his traditional Jewish roots:

This is the first: Listen Israel, the Lord our God is the one Lord, and you must love the Lord your God with all your heart, with all your soul, with all your mind, and with all your strength. (Mark 12: 29, 30)

Here was nothing about a call for belief in himself as mankind's saviour, nothing about a new religion that he wanted instituted in his name. Instead, in choosing this commandment Jesus was affirming in the most emphatic way possible that the Jewish faith was the absolute bedrock of his belief. The quotation is not just a passage from Deuteronomy (6: 4–5), it is the great *Shema Israel* (Listen Israel), the confession of faith which every practising Jew recites morning and evening every day of his life, a confession instituted by Moses in these terms:

Let these words of mine remain in your heart and in your soul; fasten them on your hand as a sign and on your forehead as a circlet. Teach them to your children and say over to them, whether at rest in your house or walking abroad, at your lying down or at your rising. Write them on the doorposts of your house, and on your gates, so that you and your children may live long in the land that God swore to your fathers he would give them for as long as there is a sky above the earth . . .

According to Mark, Jesus, without having been asked for it, then volunteered a second commandment: 'You must love your neighbour as yourself' (Mark 12: 30). Christians sometimes like to argue that here Jesus was highlighting the new twist he was bringing to the old religion, the feature by which the new faith, Christianity, would set itself apart from the traditional outlook of Judaism. Such an argument is a profound misunderstanding of what the Jewish religion had been for centuries before Jesus, and would continue to be to this day. In the commandment 'You must love your neighbour as yourself' Jesus was saying nothing new. It is first to be found in Leviticus 19: 18, one of the books attributed to Moses, and occurs again in Ecclesiasticus and in the fifth-century Tobit in the form: 'Do to no-one what you would not want done to you' (Tobit 4: 15), where it is swiftly followed by: 'Give your bread to those who are hungry, and your clothes to those who are naked'. As the German theologian Bultmann recognized, this concept was re-stated in the generation immediately before Jesus by the great Rabbi Hillel. A Gentile, weary of trying to grasp the complexities of Jewish doctrine, went to Hillel and asked him to teach him the whole of the Torah 'while I stand on one foot', i.e. briefly. Hillel told him: 'Whatever is hateful to you, do not do to your fellow-man. This is the whole Torah. The rest is commentary. Now go and study.' It is difficult therefore to believe that Jesus could ever have intended the elaborate and un-Jewish formulations of 'faith' that Nicaea and later councils devised in his name, and which still represent the way he is *supposed* to be understood by the present-day Christian.

If Jesus remained so fundamentally loyal to Judaism, how is he to be viewed by modern Jews, once all the wrong thinking and persecutions of the years following Constantine the Great are swept aside? One of the most fascinating of recent developments among Jewish writers and scholars, and not a few rabbis, has been the new interest in who Jesus was, and whether he may have been merely a *nabi/hasid* of a particularly exceptional kind.

More than fifty years ago the Jewish writer Joseph Klausner concluded his book *Jesus of Nazareth* with the words:

In his ethical code there is a sublimity, distinctiveness and originality in form unparalleled in any other Hebrew ethical code; neither is there any parallel to the remarkable art of his parables.

In 1961 the great Jewish existentialist Martin Buber wrote: 'I am more than ever certain that a great place belongs to [Jesus] in Israel's history of faith.'

Today Dr Geza Vermes goes even further, describing Jesus unequivocally as 'an unsurpassed master of the art of laying bare the inmost core of spiritual truth', and acknowledging that he was a healer 'head and shoulders' above other *hasidim* such as Hanina ben Dosa. He speaks admiringly of how:

... he took his stand among the pariahs of his world, those despised by the respectable. Sinners were his table-companions and the ostracised tax-collectors and prostitutes his friends.'

For Vermes, the one overwhelming stumbling-block is the verdict of Nicaea. In his view, Jesus 'certainly never imagined he was God. To a pious Palestinian Jew of his time, the very idea would have been inconceivable, pure blasphemy.'

Another vital point to consider is the modern Christian view of Jesus in relation to Nicaea. Ever since the German theologians first began to chip away some of the old fallacies surrounding the interpretation of Jesus' life and teaching, there has been, in some quarters at least, a tendency to ignore the areas of uncertainty. When the ideas of Strauss began to take root, and Charles Darwin unleashed his *Origin of Species*, the reaction of the contem-

The divine emperor. When a Roman emperor died he was traditionally regarded as having become a god. Here Claudius, in life a timid man with a stutter and a limp, has been transformed into Jupiter, king of the gods. From a first-century sculpture, Vatican Museum, Rome.

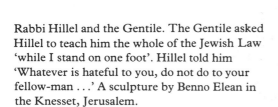

Rabbi Hillel and the Gentile. The Gentile asked Hillel to teach him the whole of the Jewish Law 'while I stand on one foot'. Hillel told him 'Whatever is hateful to you, do not do to your fellow-man . . .' A sculpture by Benno Elean in the Knesset, Jerusalem.

porary Pope, Pius IX, was to condemn rationalism and proclaim himself and all future Popes infallible. Under Pius' successor, Leo XIII, a more moderate wind blew; Catholics were encouraged to adapt to new discoveries, and in response there emerged the so-called Modernist movement, comprising Catholics prepared to view the New Testament as critically as some Protestants had done. Leading figures in this movement were the English Jesuit Father George Tyrrell and the French scholar-priest Alfred Loisy. But when, in 1903, Leo was succeeded by the altogether more reactionary Pope Pius X the relatively liberal outlook was crushed underfoot. Loisy's books were immediately banned to all Catholics. Four years later all Modernist thinking was condemned in formal decrees and encyclicals, and when, inevitably, Loisy and Tyrrell independently published protests, Tyrrell's in the form of letters to *The Times*, both were excommunicated. Tyrrell, who died two years later, was not even allowed Catholic burial, receiving interment instead in the Anglican churchyard at Storrington, West Sussex. So that no-one should lapse in the future, Pius brought in a special Anti-Modernist oath. Today, in the wake of Vatican II and with a Pope as charismatic as John Paul II, it might appear that we live in more liberal and enlightened times. But appearances can be deceptive, as demonstrated by the case of Edward Schillebeeckx.

Edward Schillebeeckx is a mild-mannered scholarly Belgian Catholic of the University of Nijmegen in the Netherlands, who has produced some prodigiously long and closely reasoned studies in which he has merely suggested that the nature of the divinity invested in Jesus at Nicaea has perhaps been over-stressed at the expense of his Jewish humanity. On Saturday, 15 December 1979, Schillebeeckx was summoned to appear before Rome's Congregation for the Doctrine of Faith, the Vatican department which in 1633 put Galileo on trial for arguing that the earth revolved around the sun. To his astonishment, as if in a scene from the Middle Ages, Schillebeeckx found himself politely but menacingly on trial for his orthodoxy, complete with the unheralded appearance as 'prosecutor' of a man who, only a month before, had accused him of totally denying Jesus' divinity. In a separate part of the same building Cardinal Franjo Seper, Prefect of the Congregation for the Doctrine of Faith, signed a declaration ending the career of the Roman Catholic Hans Küng for having questioned the idea of papal infallibility. Of such present-day auto-da-fés the most recent, and perhaps the most ironic, has been that of Archbishop Emmanuel Millingo, from Lusaka, Zambia, in March 1983. Archbishop Millingo's crime? Conducting demonstrably successful healings and exorcisms, just like those maligned Gnostics – and the founder of his faith two thousand years ago. Dealing with *mashawe*, the African word for mental stress, was reported to be the Archbishop's speciality. Regrettably, in July 1983, Millingo was obliged to resign.

It is to be acknowledged that one of the least known yet most commendable of the reforms brought about by Vatican II was the exoneration of present-day Jews from any culpability for Jesus' death, effectively erasing the last four words of the Matthew gospel's 'His blood be on us and on our children'. Yet even this, due to internecine Council wranglings, is less of a reform than it might at first appear to be. Present-day Jews can only consider themselves innocent of 'deicide' if they dissociate themselves from the 'wicked generation' of the time of Jesus. As Jewish scholar Hyam Maccoby has remarked with great justice:

> That so-called 'wicked generation' was in fact one of the greatest generations in Jewish religious history: the age of the Tannaim, of Hillel and Shammai, Johanan ben Zakkai and Gamaliel was an age in Jewish development corresponding to that of the Church Fathers in Christianity. To dissociate themselves from this generation would be, for Jews, to dissociate themselves from Judaism.

If we acknowledge that self-abnegation was a central feature of his teaching, we would expect Jesus to display a marked reluctance, as indeed he does, to assume any special title. The only one he consistently applies to himself, which no-one challenges, and which was subsequently dropped by orthodox Christianity, is 'son of man'. Much theological ink has been spilled over the exact meaning of this, but Dr Geza Vermes' interpretation is arguably the most plausible: that 'son of man' was little more than a self-deprecatory reference to himself, along the lines of 'this fellow'. If this argument is valid, then the capital letters with which it appears in modern Christian works give it precisely the opposite inference to that intended. As beautifully expressed by Dr John Robinson in his controversial *Honest to God*:

> It is in Jesus, and Jesus *alone*, that there is *nothing* of self to be seen, but *solely* the ultimate, unconditional love of God. It is as he emptied himself *utterly* of himself that he became the carrier of the 'name which is above every name.'

Jesus should be seen, then, as neither more nor less than a perfect vessel for God; nonetheless, there is one title applied to him in all the gospels, synoptic and Johannine, canonical and non-canonical, that it is difficult to deny – 'son of God'. The reason for believing that Jesus himself acknowledged this title is to be found in the parable of the wicked husbandmen, in which both the title 'son of God' and Jesus himself play an intrinsic part. It appears in all three synoptic gospels (Mark 12: 1–12; Matthew 21: 33–46; Luke 20: 9–19), and, in a particularly primitive form, in the Nag Hammadi gospel of Thomas:

He said, 'There was a good man who owned a vineyard. He leased it to tenant farmers so that they might work it and he might collect the produce from them. He sent his servant so that the tenants might give him the produce of the vineyard. They seized his servant and beat him, all but killing him. The servant went back and told his master. The master said 'Perhaps [they] did not recognize [him]'. He sent another servant. The tenants beat this one as well. Then the owner sent his son and said, 'Perhaps they will show respect to my son.' Because the tenants knew that it was he who was the heir to the vineyard, they seized him and killed him. Let him who has ears hear . . .

The meaning of the parable is quite unmistakable. The vineyard is God's earth, and the tenant farmers mankind. The servants are the Old Testament *nabi'im*, or prophets, some of whom were indeed badly treated in their time. But quite distinct from these, and suffering a far worse fate, is the individual described as 'the son'. Jesus could scarcely have more succinctly or more prophetically explained his own role in a parable drama that he would enact in his own life. And he could hardly have more plainly spelled out that his relationship with God *was* distinctive and special. But exactly how special? A Jewish historian such as Dr Vermes will quite happily acknowledge Jesus as a 'son of God' in the Jewish sense of one having a special relationship with God. Even as devout a Hindu as Mahatma Gandhi expressed his preparedness to recognize Jesus in similar terms:

To me he was one of the greatest teachers humanity has ever had. To his believers he was God's only begotten son. Could the fact that I do or do not accept this belief have any more or less influence in my life? Is all the grandeur of his teaching and his doctrine to be forbidden to me? I cannot believe so . . . My interpretation . . . is that in Jesus' own life is the key to his nearness to God; that he expressed, as no other could, the spirit and will of God. It is in this sense that I see and recognize him as the son of God.

But the Christian, the Nicene Christian at least, will demand much more, starting off the theological merry-go-round all over again. Whether he or Gandhi is right is a matter of faith. But there is an uncanny aspect to the parable of the wicked husbandmen that is relevant here: its author, a human Jew of the first century AD, essentially outlined his own excruciating path of death just as calmly and clearly as if he was seeing it through a window. Was

Left Mahatma Gandhi (1869–1948) in London in 1931 for talks on Indian independence. Although a devout Hindu, he expressed the deepest admiration for Jesus' teachings, and showed how they could be applied to the most far-reaching human problems. His devotion to Jesus stopped short of recognizing him as God, but was he or Christianity wrong?

Left Edward Schillebeeckx, of the University of Nijmegen, Netherlands. A Roman Catholic theologian, he found himself under interrogation by Rome's Congregation for the Doctrine of Faith for merely suggesting that Jesus' divinity might have been exaggerated.

Above Shema Israel! ('Listen, Israel'). When asked the first of all the commandments, Jesus unhesitatingly quoted the great *Shema*, the prayer affirming the singularity of God, which Moses instituted, and which every practising Jew recites every day of his life. The prayer is seen here on the Nash papyrus, *c*. second-century BC, until the discovery of the Dead Sea Scrolls the oldest surviving manuscript of any portion of the Hebrew Old Testament.

Jesus so completely a vessel of God, the living, breathing word of God, that to all intents and purposes God was speaking through him, and *was* him?

There is only one way of finally resolving this great dilemma: a preparedness on the part of all to recognize that in the case of Jesus, perhaps uniquely, there is no formula, no one view of him that can adequately explain or encompass him. In the course of this book we have examined Jesus the Jew, the countryman, the unconventional teacher, the exorcist and healer, the hypnotist, the victim of the Sadducees, and the mysterious Jesus of the resurrection. There is much, much more we have barely touched on, just as the author of John felt obliged to conclude:

There were many other things that Jesus did; if all were written down, the world itself, I suppose, would not hold all the books that would have to be written (John 21: 25)

The sheer futility of the Nicene Council and all others that set out to provide a formula for Christianity, has been beautifully expressed by Birmingham University lecturer Frances Young:

there are as many different responses to Jesus Christ as there are different fingerprints ... To reduce any living faith to a set of definitions and propositions one is bound to distort it. Attempts to produce creeds are inevitably divisive or compromising. Eusebius of Caesarea signed the creed of Nicaea for the sake of church unity, but he was clearly embarrassed about it. What we need is not new creeds, but a new openness which will allow manifold ways of responding and elucidating that response.

'A new openness', and casting aside of barriers. A self-abnegation. Is not this what Jesus and his kingdom of God was all about? Perhaps today's Christians should recognize that the real Jesus was more fully human than many care to contemplate. But equally, today's Jews may need to adjust to the view that God *did* speak through Jesus of Nazareth two thousand years ago, and that while he may not have seemed to be the Messiah their forbears were wanting or expecting, he was, and remains to this day, what God intended.

The following notes and bibliography are intended for readers wishing to explore further the issues raised in *Jesus: the Evidence*. In the interests of simplicity, sources appear in the notes only in an abbreviated form, except in the case of very specialized publications. Full publishing details will be found in the bibliography.

NOTES AND REFERENCES

Discovering the Documents

p 12   **Tischendorf:** For an excellent account of the discovery of Sinaiticus, and that of other early biblical manuscripts, see Deuel's *Testaments of Time*, also Tischendorf's own account *Codex Sinaiticus: Tischendorf's Story and Argument Related by Himself*.

p 13   **Dr John Covel:** See the extracts from Dr Covel's diaries in *Early Voyages* by J.T. Brent.

p 13   **Hon. Robert Curzon:** The quotation derives from his *Visit to the Monasteries*, p 366.

p 17   **Tischendorf's alleged theft of Sinaiticus:** The monks of Sinai still regard Tischendorf as having stolen their manuscript, and display a letter in which Tischendorf acknowledges he has the manuscript merely on loan (see G.H. Forsyth's 'Island of Faith', p 91). But this letter was written before the monastery had accepted a substantial payment from Tsar Nicholas, a payment negotiated by Tischendorf, apparently for the purchase of Sinaiticus. For the announcement of the British acquisition of Sinaiticus, see *The Times*, 21 December 1933, p 15.

p 17   **Technical details of Sinaiticus:** For the scholarly background, see Metzger's *Manuscripts of the Greek Bible*, pp 76-9.

p 19   **Oxyrhynchus excavations:** The quotation from Grenfell derives from his article 'The Oldest Record ...', p 1030. For details of the other manuscript fragments discovered by Grenfell and Hunt, see their multi-volume *The Oxyrhynchus Papyri* published by the Egyptian Exploration Fund. Their work was carried on by others after their deaths.

p 22   **Chester Beatty collection:** News of the Chester Beatty acquisition was announced in an article by Sir Frederic George Kenyon, *The Times*, 19 November 1931, p 13. See also Kenyon's *The Chester Beatty Biblical Papyri* for a definitive appraisal. The exact location where the papyri were found remains unknown.

p 22 **Nag Hammadi discovery:** The manuscripts were almost certainly originally hidden by someone from the nearby monastery of St Pachomius. For background on the whole story, and an appraisal of the manuscripts themselves see Elaine Pagels' *The Gnostic Gospels*. Full translations of the manuscripts are to be found in James M. Robinson's *The Nag Hammadi Library*, from which the Gospel of Thomas and other extracts quoted in this book are derived.

p 26 **Morton Smith:** For the definitive account of his Secret Gospel findings, see his *Clement of Alexandria and a Secret Gospel of Mark*. For a general account, see his *The Secret Gospel*. Some scholars accept Professor Smith's claims; others view them with considerable reservations.

p 28 **Egerton Papyrus 2:** A full translation and definitive appraisal is to be found in Bell and Skeat's *Fragments of an Unknown Gospel*. In the extract quoted I have modernized Bell and Skeat's 'Biblical' English.

p 29 **Rylands Papyrus:** See C.H. Roberts' *An Unpublished Fragment....*

p 31 **Quotation from Bruce Metzger:** This derives from his 'Recently Published Greek Papyri ...', p 38.

The Fallibility of the Gospels

p 32 **Manuscript punctuation, dating, etc:** For a lucid, modern summary of the technical details, see Metzger *Manuscripts of the Greek Bible*.

p 34 **Parallel passage technique:** For examples of this technique as applied to the synoptic gospels, see Throckmorton *Gospel Parallels*.

p 35 **Reimarus' 'On the Aims of Jesus ...':** The original German title of Reimarus' work was *Von dem Zwecke Jesu und seiner Jünger*. This was the last of the so-called Wolfenbüttel Fragments, published by G.E. Lessing after Reimarus' death. (See Lessing in bibliography.)

p 35 **Strauss' 'The Life of Jesus ...':** The original German title of Strauss' work was *Das Leben Jesu*. The first English language version, translated by George Eliot, was published in 1846.

p 36 **F.C. Baur:** Although Baur's output was prodigious, only two of his works have been translated into English, *Paul the Apostle of Jesus Christ* (1873-5) and *The Church History of the First Three Centuries* (1878-9). For an excellent appraisal of his significance, see Stephen Neill's *The Interpretation of the New Testament*, pp 19-28.

p 36 **Holtzmann and priority of the Mark gospel:** For the part played by Holtzmann in establishing the Mark gospel's priority, see Kümmel's *Introduction to the New Testament*, p 151. Its priority has been challenged in recent years by W.R. Farmer (see bibliography), who has reverted to the original Griesbach interpretation that the Mark gospel is a conflation of Matthew's and Luke's.

p 36 **Mark as secretary or interpreter for Peter:** According to the second-century bishop Papias, as quoted in Eusebius' *History of the Church*, book 3 –

This, too, the presbyter used to say: 'Mark, who had been Peter's interpreter, wrote down carefully, but not in order, all that he remembered of the Lord's sayings and doings. For he had not heard the Lord, or been one of his followers, but later, as I said, one of Peter's ...'   Eusebius' *History*, trans. Williamson, p 152

p 37   **John gospel written at Ephesus:** This is attested by, among others, the early Church father Irenaeus (*c* 130–*c* 200 AD).

p 37   **Wrede:** The original German title of Wrede's book was *Das Messiasgeheimnis in den Evangelien*, published at Göttingen in 1901. It has never been translated into English, but for a summary of its content, see William Sanday's *The Life of Christ in Recent Research*.

p 37   **Schweitzer:** The original German title of Schweitzer's book was *Von Reimarus zu Wrede*, published in 1905. The quotation derives from the English language edition, p 396.

p 38   **Bultmann:** For Bultmann's own elucidation of the principles of form criticism, see his *Die Geschichte der synoptischen Tradition*, 1921, published in English as *The History of the Synoptic Tradition*, 1963.

p 39   **Quotation from Bultmann:** This derives from his *Jesus and the Word*, p 14.

p 39   **Dr Vermes on the Bultmann school:** The comment derives from Vermes 'Quest for the historical Jesus', *Jewish Chronicle Literary Supplement*, 12 December 1969.

p 40   **Don Cupitt:** Don Cupitt's remarks on the *zakkau/dakkau* misreading, to which I am indebted, derive from his *Who Was Jesus?*, pp 52, 53.

p 41   **Manual of Discipline:** The quotation derives from Vermes' *The Dead Sea Scrolls in English*, p 93.

p 44   **Early Aramaic element in the John gospel:** According to Burney, speaking of himself –

... the writer turned seriously to tackle the question of the original language of the Fourth Gospel; and quickly convincing himself that the theory of an original Aramaic document was no chimera, but a fact which was capable of the fullest verification, set himself to collect and classify the evidence in a form which he trusts may justify the reasonableness of his opinion not merely to other Aramaic scholars, but to all New Testament scholars who will take the pains to follow out his arguments. (Burney's *The Aramaic Origin of the Fourth Gospel*, p 3)

Olmstead somewhat arbitrarily separated the narrative and discourse elements of the gospel, arguing that the former represented the earliest and most authentic source of biographical information on Jesus. Variants of the same argument have subsequently been adopted by Professor Charles H. Dodd in his *Historical Tradition in the Fourth Gospel* (see especially p 120), and by Dr John A.T. Robinson in his *Redating the New Testament*.

p 44   **The 'Gabbatha' or Pavement:** For the arguments identifying the Sion convent pavement with that referred to by the writer of the John gospel, see Fr L.H. Vincent's 'Le lithostrotos évangelique', also P. Benoit's 'Prétoire, Lithostroton et Gabbatha'.

p 44   · **Quotation from Papias:** See Eusebius, *op. cit.*, p 153.

p 46   **Professor Brandon and pro-Roman slant of Mark gospel:** See Professor Brandon's *The Fall of Jerusalem and the Christian Church*.

p 48   **Kümmel dating of gospels:** See his *Introduction to the New Testament*.

p 49   **Quotation from Nicholas Sherwin-White:** This derives from p 191 of *Roman Society and Roman Law in the New Testament*.

Did Jesus Even Exist?

p 51   **John Allegro and Professor G. A. Wells:** For details of the works of these writers, see bibliography. John Allegro was forcefully refuted in *The Times*, 26 May 1970, and an acerbic review of Wells' *Did Jesus Exist?*, written by Dr John Robinson, appeared in the October 1976 *Journal of Theological Studies*, pp 447–9.

p 54   **Jesus' human appearance:** Often quoted as a contemporary description of Jesus is the so-called 'Letter of Lentulus', purporting to have been sent from one Lentulus 'president of the people of Jerusalem' to the Senate in Rome. There was no such office as 'president of the people of Jerusalem', and the letter, first known from the writings of the eleventh-century St Anselm, may be confidently dismissed as a late forgery. See Farrar's *The Life of Christ Represented in Art*, p 84.

p 55   **Census of Quirinius:** For a definitive appraisal of the Luke gospel's deficiencies concerning this census, see Excursus I 'The Census of Quirinius', in Schürer's *History of the Jewish People* (1973 edition), pp 400–27.

p 56   **Kepler:** Kepler's original book describing his astronomical findings was *De Jesu Christi Salvatoris Nostri Vero Anno Natalitio*, published in 1606.

p 56   **Clark, Parkinson and Stephenson:** See bibliography.

p 56   **Solar Calendar theory:** See A. Jaubert's *The Date of the Last Supper*.

p 58   **Tacitus:** The reference to 'Christ' occurs in his *Annals of Imperial Rome*, book 15, 44. See Penguin translation by Michael Grant, p 354.

p 58   **Suetonius:** The full reference reads 'Because the Jews at Rome caused continuous disturbances at the instigation of Chrestus, he [Claudius] expelled them from the city.' (*The Twelve Caesars*, Penguin translated by Robert Graves, p 197)

p 58   **Pliny:** The reference to Christians derives from his Letters, x, 96–7. For the full text of the letter, see B. J. Kidd's *Documents Illustrative of the History of the Church*, vol I, 1920, no. 14.

p 61   **Josephus on Jesus:** The passage describing Jesus as a 'wise man' occurs in *Antiquities* XX, 3, 3 (63–4). The reference to James as brother of Jesus derives from *Antiquities* XX, 9, 1 (200–3). For a definitive appraisal of these passages, and the extent to which they have suffered alteration, see Excursus II 'Josephus on Jesus and James' in Schürer's *History of the Jewish People*, pp 428–41.

p 61   **Origen on Josephus and Jesus:** See his *Comm. in Matthaeum*, 10, 17 (referring to Matthew 13: 55); also *Contra Celsum*, 1, 47. Origen provides crucial corroboration that Josephus did refer to Jesus, but did not believe he was the Messiah, or Christ.

p 61   **Agapius on Josephus:** See Shlomo Pines' *An Arabic Version of the Testimonium Flavianum and its Implications*.

pp 62,   **Quotations from Baraitha and Tosefta:** These derive as follows –
63   1 Baraitha, *Babylonian Talmud*, Sanhedrin 43a
            2 ditto

3 Tosefta, *Hullin (Profane Things)* II, 22, 23
4 Tosefta, *Hullin* II, 24

For the fullest discussion of these extracts, see Rabbi Goldstein's *Jesus in the Jewish Tradition*, especially pp 22–51.

p 64   **Pantera, Panthera:** For a full discussion, with sources, see Goldstein, *op. cit.*, pp 35–9.

p 64   **Origen's reference to Panthera:** As quoted by Origen, this reads –

> Mary was turned out by her husband, a carpenter by profession, after she had been convicted of unfaithfulness. Cast off by her spouse, and wandering about in disgrace, she then in obscurity gave birth to Jesus by a certain soldier Panthera. (Origen *Contra Celsum*, refutation 1, 28)

p 64   **Panthera tombstone:** For a full appraisal see A. Deissmann's *Light from the Ancient East*, pp 74, 75.

Jesus, the Jew

p 66   **Jesus' education:** The Luke gospel story of Jesus astonishing the doctors in the Temple (Luke 2: 41–50) should be regarded with some scepticism. Josephus tells a very similar story of himself at the age of fourteen. But there is no reason to believe Jesus was not well-educated. As theologian C.F.D. Moule remarked –

> It seems fair to assume that, broadly speaking, the average Jew was better educated than the average Gentile, if only because Jewish family life was the soundest in the empire, and also the education which Jewish children received in the synagogue school was, within its limits, probably more conscientious and thorough than the teaching given by Gentile schoolmasters who had not necessarily the intensity of vocation belonging to a devout teacher of the Torah. (C.F.D. Moule's *The Birth of the New Testament*, p 157)

p 67   **Quotation from Rabbi Goldstein:** See his *Jesus in the Jewish Tradition*, p 24.

p 67   **Gospel reference to Nazareth:** In the Mark gospel, already noted as most likely the earliest, specific reference to Nazareth occurs only in chapter 1, verse 9. In four later passages (Mark 1: 24; 10: 47; 14: 67 and 16: 6), the original Greek refers to Jesus as 'the Nazarene'.

p 67   **Nazareth excavations and inscription:** Archaeological findings of early settlement at Nazareth are described in C. Kopp's *The Holy Places of the Gospels*, pp 60–1. The Nazareth inscription is published in M. Avi-Yonah's article 'A List of Priestly Courses from Caesarea'.

p 67   **Josephus reference to Capharnaum:** This derives from his *Jewish War*, book III, 521, Penguin translation by Williamson, p 231.

p 70   **Jesus the countryman:** For Dr Geza Vermes' remarks on Jesus as a *campagnard*, see his *Jesus the Jew*, pp 48, 49.

p 70   **Quotation from Talmud:** This derives from the Babylonian Talmud, '*Erubin* 53b. See also Vermes *op. cit.*, p 52.

p 70   **References to 'Eleazar', 'Lazar' and 'Laze':** For description of a Jerusalem ossuary bearing the name 'Eleazar', see *Gli scavi del 'Dominus Flevit'* I, Tipographia dei P. Franciscani, Jerusalem, 1958, p 92. For examples of 'Lazar' and 'Laze' at Beth She'arim, see M. Schwabe and B. Lifshitz *Beth She'arim* II, no. 177, p 73; no. 93, p 34.

p 71   **Eusebius' reference to arrest of Jesus' relatives:** See Eusebius *History*, III, 20, Williamson trans., pp 126, 127.

p 72   **Humility:** It is important to note that in pagan countries this concept was so foreign that there was not even a word for it. The Greek word used in biblical texts has the connotation 'abject', or 'contemptible' among most pagan authors. See E.R. Dodds' *The Greeks and the Irrational* (University of California Press, Berkeley, 1951), p 215.

p 74   **Nabi/Nabi'im:** Dr Geza Vermes has pointed out that a technically more correct rendition of the plural is 'nebi'im'. 'Nabi'im' has however been adopted in order to avoid confusion.

p 78   **David and Bathsheba:** For biblical references, see 2 Samuel, chapters 11 and 12. Note that Nathan points out David's sinfulness by means of a parable that is a direct prototype for the parables of Jesus.

p 78   **Excavations at Giv'at ha-Mivtar:** See the definitive article by N. Haas 'Anthropological Observations on the Skeletal Remains from Giv'at ha-Mivtar'.

p 80   **Intense separatism of first-century Jewish religion:** Deserving of quotation are remarks by Hugh J. Schonfield –

> ... in those days Judaism was not so much a creed as a way of life of the Jewish people based on the Divine Laws, the Torah, laid down in the books of Moses. The dogmatic element was essentially confined to belief in the Unity of God and the claim that Israel had been chosen as the vehicle of the Divine will to mankind. Everything else was a matter of group thinking, persuasion and interpretation. (Schonfield's *Pentecost Revolution*, p 249)

p 80   **Excavation of priestly houses:** See Yigael Yadin's *Jerusalem Revealed*.

p 83   **Honi the Circle Drawer and Hanina ben Dosa:** For detailed information on these and similar early *hasidim*, see Vermes' *Jesus the Jew*, pp 69–82.

p 83   **Messiah's non-awareness of own identity:** According to the words Justin Martyr put into the mouth of the Jew Trypho, 'Even though the Messiah has been born and is living somewhere, yet he is still unknown. Indeed, he does not even know himself, nor has he any power until Elijah comes, anoints him, and reveals him to all.' (Justin Martyr's *Dialogue with Trypho*, 8)

Flouter of Convention

p 84   **Quotation from Josephus on John the Baptist:** This derives from *Antiquities* 18, 116–19.

p 86   **W.F. Albright on Aenon near Salim:** The quotation derives from Albright's *The Archaeology of Palestine*, p 247.

p 86 **Nudity in early Christian baptism:** As pointed out in Morton Smith's *Clement of Alexandria*, pp 175, 176, nudity in baptism was prescribed in Hippolytus' *Apostolic Tradition* XXI, 3, 5, 11, and was required by the Pharisees in their baptism of proselytes and immersion for purification (Mikwa'ot 8 and 9; *B. Yebamot* 47b). It is implicit in Paul's reference to 'complete stripping' in Colossians 2: 11. In the earliest Christian art, where Jesus' baptism is a common theme, he is invariably represented quite naked. Such nudity does not contradict the traditional association of a white garment with baptism, symbolic of a burial shroud, and cast aside at the moment of baptismal 'rebirth'. For baptism as a form of 'death', see Paul's letter to the Romans (Romans 6: 3–5).

p 87 **How any Jew could be 'son of God':** In his *Jesus the Man and the Myth* James Mackey has pointed out that any Jew, '. . . if unusually faithful to the will of God in this world, could claim to be Son of God in that sense, and have the claim allowed. In the Judaea royal ritual the king was declared son of God on his enthronement' (Mackey's *Jesus the Man and the Myth*, p 65). For the association of this title with the royal ritual, see 2 Samuel 7, and Psalm 2.

p 87 **Initiations in Greek magical papyri:** See Morton Smith's *Jesus the Magician*, p 103.

p 88 **Quotation from Josephus:** This derives from *Antiquities* 18, 117–18.

p 88 **Feeding of the five thousand:** For Dr John Robinson's observations on this passage, see his *Can We Trust the New Testament?*, p 92.

p 88 **That Mark drew on two separate accounts of the feeding of the five thousand:** The Mark gospel author quotes two separate accounts of the feeding of large crowds, one of five thousand (6: 30–44), the other of four thousand (8: 1–10). As pointed out by Dr Vincent Taylor in *The Gospel According to St Mark* (London, 1966), it seems unlikely that these were two separate incidents, particularly since in the second the disciples ask 'Where could anyone get bread to feed these people in a deserted place like this?', thus apparently ignorant of the first occasion, which they were reported to have witnessed. The sensible explanation is that Mark was working from two slightly different *written* versions of a single incident. Had his sources been verbal, he would have been more likely to recognize their common ancestry.

p 89 **'Abba':** There are considerable scholastic differences about the significance of Jesus' use of this word. Some have argued it to be the equivalent of our 'Daddy'. Jewish scholars such as Vermes, however, point out that it could be used both formally and as an expression of familiarity. It is to be noted that when Jesus began the so-called 'Lord's Prayer' (Matthew 6: 9–13) with the words 'Our Father which art in heaven', he was following the pattern of Pharisee prayer which still forms part of the Jewish Daily Prayer Book.

p 89 **Tetragrammaton:** For an introduction to the use of this in early manuscripts, see Metzger's *Manuscripts of the Greek Bible*, pp 33–5.

p 89 **'Abba' addressed to God by Honi's grandson:** Honi the Circle Drawer's grandson was a *hasid* by the name of Hanan. For his usage of 'Abba' see Babylonian Talmud *Ta'anith (Fasting)* 23b, also Vermes' *Jesus the Jew*, p 211.

p 92 **Josephus on Essenes:** The reference to Essene attitudes to possessions, weapons, footwear, etc., derive from his *Jewish War*, book II, 125 ff., Penguin translation by Williamson, p 133.

p 94   **Yose the Galilean:** This story derives from the Babylonian Talmud *'Erubin* 53b.

p 96   **Suggestion of Jesus' homosexuality:** See Hugh Montefiore's 'Jesus, the Revelation of God'.

p 96   **Quotation from 'Gospel of Philip':** See J. M. Robinson's *The Nag Hammadi Library*, p 138.

p 97   **Suggestion of Jesus as libertine:** For Morton Smith on this angle, see *The Secret Gospel*, pp 114, 140, in which he imputes a sexual element to Jesus' secret baptism. This would appear to be pure mischief-making on Smith's part, with no serious evidence to support it.

Man of Miracles

p 99   **Jewish memory of Jesus as healer/sorcerer:** That Jesus' 'miracles' remained in Jewish folk-memory long after the crucifixion is indicated by several Talmud passages describing cures performed long after his death by means of charms inscribed with his name. See Tosefta, *Hullin* II, 22; *B.Av.Zar.* 27b; *Y.Av.Zar.* II, 40d; *Y.Sabb.* XIV, 14d.

p 100   **Quotation from Canon Anthony Harvey:** This derives from his *Jesus and the Constraints of History*, p 110.

p 100   **Excavations at Sheep Pool:** For an excellent, detailed account of these, and the literature surrounding the site, see Jack Finegan's *The Archaeology of the New Testament*, pp 142–7. See also J. Jeremias 'The Rediscovery of Bethesda'. The names Bethzatha/Bezetha/Bethesda, etc., all appear to denote the same site.

p 100   **Quotation from the Bordeaux pilgrim:** This is a translation of the Latin original published in P. Geyer's *Corpus Scriptorum Ecclesiasticorum Latinorum*, vol 39, p 21 (Vienna 1889).

p 102   **Stress as causative factor in hysterical illnesses:** For a medical appraisal of this, and discussion of the efficacy of hypnosis in the treatment of, for instance, stress-induced skin disorders, see Gordon Ambrose and George Newbold's *Handbook of Medical Hypnosis*, especially chapter 13.

p 103   **Reptilian skin-disorder:** For a detailed medical account of the successful use of hypnosis in this case, see Dr A.A. Mason's 'A Case of Congenital Ichthyosiform Erythrodermia of Brocq Treated by Hypnosis', *British Medical Journal*, 23 August 1952, pp 422, 423.

p 106   **Dr F. Ray Bettley:** For Dr Bettley's comments on the case treated by Dr Mason, see his letter in the 1952 *British Medical Journal*, vol II, p 996.

p 106   **Professor Lionel Haward, and ancient Egyptian use of hypnosis:** See Professor Haward's lecture 'Hypnosis in the Service of Research', p 2, also F.L. Griffith and H. Thompson's *The Demotic Magical Papyrus of London and Leiden*. According to Professor Haward, this describes the technique of self-hypnosis using a light source. British Museum Egyptologists have expressed some scepticism on Professor Haward's interpretation, but there can be little doubt that induction of trance states was a common feature in early religion, and hypnosis provides a convenient label for this process.

p 107   **Quotation from Professor Oesterreich:** This derives from the English language edition of his *Possession, Demoniacal and Other*, p 5.

p 107   **West Yorkshire 'possession' case:** For accounts of the trial associated with this, see *The Times*, 22 to 24 April 1975, also *The Yorkshire Post* of the same dates.

p 107   **Christopher Neil-Smith:** See his *The Exorcist and the Possessed*, listed in the bibliography.

p 107   **Multiple personality cases:** There is a growing literature on this subject. Chris Sizemore has written her autobiography under the title *Eve* (see bibliography, Sizemore and Pittillo); U.S. author Daniel Keyes has written an account of the Billy Milligan case in *The Minds of Billy Milligan*; Flora Rheta Schreiber has graphically recreated the problems of a pseudonymous East Coast American art student in *Sybil*, first published in the U.K. by Allen Lane in 1974.

p 108   **'Unclean spirits':** For the view that ascription of disease to 'unclean spirits' was particularly associated with Galilean Pharisee rabbis as distinct from Judaean rabbis, see Herbert Loewe's 'Demons and Spirits (Jewish)' in *The Encyclopaedia of Religion and Ethics*. Judaean rabbis specialized more in the use of roots and herbs.

p 113   **Gershom Scholem:** See his *Trends in Jewish Mysticism*, also *The Messianic Idea in Judaism* in which, on p 182, he refers to a visionary 'ascent of the soul' to heaven claimed by the eighteenth-century Jewish mystic, the Baal Shem.

Why Was He Killed?

p 114   **Jesus as militant nationalist:** See S.G.F. Brandon's *Jesus and the Zealots*, Hyam Maccoby's *Revolution in Judaea*, and Joel Carmichael's *The Death of Jesus*. For Dr Geza Vermes' views on this subject, see his *Jesus the Jew*, pp 49, 50.

p 116   **Entry into Jerusalem:** The interpretation of Jesus' actions in this instance is derived from Canon Anthony Harvey's *Jesus and the Constraints of History*. It is to be acknowledged, however, that this interpretation is regarded with some scepticism by Dr Vermes.

p 120   **Gethsemane:** The word is Hebrew for 'oil press'.

p 120   **Dr Frederick Zugibe on haematidrosis:** See his *The Cross and the Shroud*, pp 2–13.

p 121   **Trial of Jesus:** For a Jewish interpretation of this, see Paul Winter's *On the Trial of Jesus*. Classical historians have similarly suggested that the trial was a mere clandestine interrogation by Temple officials. Pilate's actions the next day are also regarded as makeshift and informal. See the report on a Cambridge lecture by F.G.B. Millar in *The Times* of 30 July 1971, p 3.

p 121   **High priest's tearing of robes:** This appears to be a contemporary gesture of despair, see also Acts 14: 14. The rending of the veil of the Temple at Jesus' death (Mark 15: 38) seems to have been injected into the gospel story as a sign of God's despair at the Jewish people's rejection of Jesus.

p 122   **Acclamation of Bar Kokhba as Messiah:** For the full quotation, with sources, see Yadin *Bar Kokhba*, p 255.

p 122   **Quotation from Rabbi Goldstein:** See his *Jesus in the Jewish Tradition*, p 26.

p 122   **Temple death penalty notices:** The inscription on these notices reads 'Let no foreigner enter within the screen and enclosure surrounding the Sanctuary. Whoever is taken so doing will be the cause that death overtakes him' (Deissmann's

Light from the Ancient East, p 80). That this meant death at Jewish hands is quite clear from the words Josephus puts into the mouth of the Roman commander Titus when reproving the participants in the Jewish Revolt –

> You disgusting people! Didn't you put up that balustrade [on the Temple] to guard your Holy House? Didn't you at intervals along it place slabs incribed in Greek characters and our own forbidding anyone to go beyond the parapet? And didn't we give you leave to execute anyone who did go beyond it, even if he was a Roman? (Josephus *Jewish War*, book 6, 136, Penguin translation by Williamson, p 347)

p 123 **Pilate dedicatory inscription:** For a full discussion of the inscription, see Carla Brusa Gerra's *Scavi di Caesarea Maritima*, pp 217-20.

pp 123, 124 **Josephus on Jewish passive resistance:** The quotations derive from *The Jewish War*, Williamson translation, pp 138, 139.

p 126 **Josephus on Jesus' sentencing by Pilate:** For source, see note for p 69.

p 128 **Dr Yigael Yadin:** For his comments on the Giv'at ha-Mivtar crucifixion remains, see his article 'Epigraphy and Crucifixion'.

p 128 **Dr Moller-Christensen's reconstruction:** See his article 'Skeletal Remains . . .' (see bibliography).

p 128 **Quotation from Dr Nicu Haas:** This derives from his article 'Anthropological Observations . . .', p 57 (see bibliography).

p 131 **The Turin Shroud:** This is a lively literature for and against its authenticity. See my own *The Turin Shroud* for a review of the subject as understood up to 1978. Arguments against the cloth's authenticity can sometimes be as subjective as those in favour: see, for instance, Joe Nickell's recent *Inquest on the Shroud of Turin*.

p 134 **Ossuary burials:** For details of these as discovered at Giv'at ha-Mivtar, see V. Tzaferis' 'Jewish Tombs at and near Giv'at ha-Mivtar'.

p 134 **Quotation from Socrates Scholasticus:** This derives from his *History of the Church*, 1, 17, English translation by A.C. Zenos, *Nicene and Post-Nicene Christian Fathers*, Ser. 2, vol 2 (Oxford 1890).

p 136 **Kathleen Kenyon's Jerusalem excavations:** See her *Jerusalem, Excavating 3,000 Years of History*.

The Empty Tomb Mystery

p 137 **The Gallio Inscription:** For a full discussion of this, see Deissmann's *St Paul, A Study in Social and Religious History*, Appendix I, pp 244 ff.

p 140 **D.H. Lawrence's 'The Man Who Died':** Originally published in 1929 as 'The Escaped Cock', this is readily available in Penguin Books' collection of Lawrence short stories, *Love Among the Haystacks and other stories* (1960 edition), pp 125-73.

p 140 **Tomb of Jesus at Srinagar:** For a Muslim viewpoint, see Muhammed Zafrulla Khan's *Deliverance from the Cross*, pp 102, 103.

p 140 **Strauss' 'A New Life of Jesus':** This was Strauss' second treatise on Jesus, originally published in German under the title *Das Leben Jesu für das deutsche Volk* *bearbeitet*. The quotation derives from the English edition, vol I, p 412, published in 1879.

p 140 **History of Religion School:** This is more correctly termed the Religiongeschicht-liche Schule, since most of its members were German.

p 141 **Forcible conversion of Galilee:** For details, see Josephus' *Antiquities*, book XII, 9, I and book XIII.

pp 141, **Quotation concerning hypnotized housewife:** This derives from Colin Wilson's
142 *Mysteries*, pp 302, 303.

p 142 **Dieter Georgi:** Although this hypothesis by Dieter Georgi has been supported by Professor Helmut Koester, it seems quite unnecessarily far-fetched, particularly in view of the gospel stories' insistence that the stone of Jesus' tomb had been rolled aside, and the body discovered to be gone.

p 144 **Dr William Sargant on Paul:** See his *Battle for the Mind*, pp 105, 106. Sargant describes Paul's experience as 'the most striking and momentous conversion ... recorded in the Acts in terms consonant with modern physiological observations'.

p 145 **Professor Brandon on St Paul:** See in particular his *History Today* article, 'Saint Paul: The Problem Figure of Primitive Christianity'.

p 148 **'Gospel of Thomas' reference to James:** 'The disciples said to Jesus. We know that you will depart from us. Who is to be our leader? Jesus said to them "Wherever you are, you are to go to James the Righteous ..." ' (J.M. Robinson *Nag Hammadi Library*, p 119).

p 149 **Hegesippus' reference to James:** An extensive extract from Hegesippus' writings on James has been preserved in Eusebius' *History of the Church*, book 2, ch. 23. See Penguin edition, trans. Williamson, pp 99-102.

p 149 **Josephus on James:** This derives from Josephus' *Antiquities* XX, 9, I.

p 152 **Date of Masada's fall:** This has been dated by most scholars, including archaeologist Yadin, to the spring of 73 AD. But from inscriptions found some twenty-five years ago in Italy, the Roman general Silva did not leave Rome for Judaea until 73 AD, which would have left no time for the siege to be organized and brought to a conclusion in that year. As now generally agreed, Masada's fall was most likely in 74 AD.

p 152 **'Gospel according to the Hebrews' reference to Jesus appearing to James:** 'Now the Lord, when he had given the *sindon* [shroud] to the servant of the priest, went to James and appeared to him ...' ('Gospel according to the Hebrews', as quoted in St Jerome *De Viris Illustribus*, ch. 2).

p 155 **World's earliest church building?** For a discussion of the structure found under St Peter's, and its possible use for early baptisms, see John Walsh *The Bones of St Peter*, pp 142-6.

How He Became God

p 157 **Constantine and Nicaea:** For a detailed, yet highly readable account of Constantine's rise to power, and the proceedings at Nicaea, see John Holland Smith's *Constantine the Great*.

p 162 **Mosaic from Mausoleum of the Julii:** The discovery of this mosaic is described in John Walsh's *The Bones of St Peter*, pp 25-7.

p 162 **Constantine's naked baptism:** See Smith, *op. cit.*, p 294.

p 164 **Quotations from Clement of Alexandria and Athanasius:** The Clement passage derives from his *Stromateis* 6, 9; that of Athanasius from his *De Incarnatione* 16: 18. I owe these quotations to a footnote in Dr John Robinson's *The Human Face of God*, p 39.

p 165 **Letter of Constantine to Arius and Alexander:** See Smith, *op. cit.*, pp 191, 192.

p 166 **Nicaea theology:** For a clear and concise explanation of the theological issues debated at Nicaea, see Don Cupitt's *The Debate about Christ*, pp 1-5.

p 168 **Eusebius of Caesarea's letter to his home diocese:** This letter is preserved in Socrates Scholasticus' *History of the Church*, 1, 8. For English translation, see note, p 184.

p 172 **Quotation 'Understand now by this present statute …':** This derives from Constantine's letter on the heretics, preserved in Eusebius' *Life of Constantine*, 2, pp 64-5. For full text in English, see *Library of the Nicene Fathers*, vol 1.

The Real Jesus

p 178 **Quotation from Martin Buber:** This is derived from his *Two Types of Faith*, p 13.

p 178 **Quotations from Dr Geza Vermes:** The first two comments derive from his *Jesus the Jew*, p 224.

p 180 **Protests by Tyrrell and Loisy:** Tyrrell's protest took the form of letters to *The Times*, published 30 September and 1 October 1907. Loisy made his objections in book form, *Simples Réflexions*, published in 1908, and his definitive work *Les Evangiles Synoptiques*.

p 180 **Edward Schillebeeckx:** For background to his life and thought, see John Bowden's *Edward Schillebeeckx, Portrait of a Theologian*.

p 181 **Archbishop Millingo:** See reports in the *Sunday Times* of 6 March and 8 August 1983.

p 181 **Quotation from Hyam Maccoby:** This derives from his *The Sacred Executioner*, p 20.

p 181 **Dr Vermes on the 'son of man':** See his *Jesus the Jew*, ch. 7.

p 181 **Quotation from Dr John Robinson:** This derives from his controversial *Honest to God*, p 74.

p 182 **Quotation from 'Gospel of Thomas':** This is Logion 65, as published in J.M. Robinson's *The Nag Hammadi Library*, pp 125, 126.

p 182 **Quotation from Gandhi:** This derives from Gandhi's *What Jesus Means to Me*, compiled by R.K. Prabhu (Navajivan Publishing House, Ahmadabad 1959), pp 9 and 10.

p 184 **Quotation from Frances Young:** This derives from her article 'A Cloud of Witnesses', published in *The Myth of God Incarnate*, ed. John Hick, p 38.

BIBLIOGRAPHY

ALBRIGHT, W.F., *The Archaeology of Palestine* (Penguin Books, Harmondsworth, revised ed., 1956)

ALLEGRO, J., *The Sacred Mushroom and the Cross* (Hodder & Stoughton, London, 1970)

AMBROSE, G. & NEWBOLD, G., *A Handbook of Medical Hypnosis* (Bailliere Tindall & Cassell, London, 1968)

AVI-YONAH, M., 'A list of Priestly Courses from Caesarea' (*Israel Exploration Journal* 12, 1962, pp 137-9)

BAIGENT, M., LEIGH, R. & LINCOLN, H., *The Holy Blood and the Holy Grail* (Jonathan Cape, London, 1982)

BELL, H.I. & SKEAT, T.C., *Fragments of an Unknown Gospel* (British Museum, London, 1935)

BENOIT, P., 'Prétoire, Lithostroton et Gabbatha' (*Revue Biblique* 59, Paris, 1952, pp 531-50)

BOWDEN, J., *Edward Schillebeeckx, Portrait of a Theologian* (SCM, London, 1983)

BRANDON, S.G.F., *The Fall of Jerusalem and the Christian Church* (SPCK, London, 1951)
'Saint Paul, the Problem Figure of Christianity' (*History Today*, October 1961)
Jesus and the Zealots (Manchester University Press, 1967)
The Trial of Jesus of Nazareth (Batsford, London, 1968)

BRENT, J.T. (ed.), 'Extracts from the Diaries of Dr John Covel 1670-1679', *Early Voyages and Travels in the Levant* (Hakluyt Society, 87, 1893, pp 101-287)

BUBER, M., *Two Types of Faith* (Harper Torch Books, New York, 1961)

BULTMANN, R., *Jesus and the Word* (Scribner, New York, 1958)
The History of the Synoptic Tradition (Oxford University Press, 1963)

BURNEY, C.F., *The Aramaic Origin of the Fourth Gospel* (Clarendon Press, Oxford, 1922)

CARMICHAEL, J., *The Death of Jesus* (Victor Gollancz, London, 1963)

CLARK, D., PARKINSON, J. & STEPHENSON, R., 'An Astronomical Re-Appraisal of the Star of Bethlehem. A Nova in 5 BC' (*Quarterly Journal of the Royal Astronomical Society* 18, 1977, p 443)

CUPITT, D. & ARMSTRONG, P., *Who Was Jesus?* (BBC, London, 1977)

CUPITT, D., *The Debate about Christ* (SCM, London, 1979)

CURZON, R., *A Visit to the Monasteries in the Levant* (Reprint with intro. by D.G. Hogarth: Humphrey Milford, London, 1916)

DEISSMANN, A., *St Paul, A Study in Social and Religious History* (trans. L.R.M. Strachan: Hodder & Stoughton, London, 1912)
Light from the Ancient East, The New Testament Illustrated by Recently Discovered Texts of the Graeco-Roman World (Hodder & Stoughton, London, 1927)

DEUEL, L., *Testaments of Time. The Search for Lost Manuscripts and Records* (Secker & Warburg, London, 1966)

DODD, C.H., *Historical Tradition in the Fourth Gospel* (Cambridge University Press, 1963)

EUSEBIUS OF CAESAREA, *The History of the Church from Christ to Constantine* (trans. G.A. Williamson: Penguin Books, Harmondsworth, 1965)

FARMER, W.R., *The Synoptic Problem* (Macmillan, London & New York, 1964)

FARRAR, F.W., *The Life of Christ as Represented in Art* (A & C Black, London, 1901)

FINEGAN, J., *The Archaeology of the New Testament* (Princeton University Press, 1969)

FORSYTH, G.H., 'Island of Faith in the Sinai Wilderness' (*National Geographic Magazine* 125, January 1964)

GERRA, C.B., 'Le Inscrizioni', *Scavi di Caesarea Maritima* ('L'Erma' di Bretschneider, Rome, 1966)

GOLDSTEIN, M., *Jesus in the Jewish Tradition* (Macmillan, New York, 1950)

GRENFELL, B.P., 'The Oldest Record of Christ. The First Complete Account of the "Sayings of Our Lord"'. Intro. by F.G. Kenyon (*McClure's* 11, 1897, pp 1022–30)

GRENFELL, B.P. & HUNT, A.S., et al., *The Oxyrhynchus Papyri*, vols 1–25 (Egypt Exploration Fund, Graeco-Roman Branch, London, 1898–1959)

GRIFFITH, F.L. & THOMPSON, H., *The Demotic Magical Papyrus of London and Leiden* (Clarendon Press, Oxford, 1921)

GUILDING, A., *The Fourth Gospel and Jewish Worship* (Oxford University Press, 1960)

HAAS, N., 'Anthropological Observations on the Skeletal Remains from Giv'at ha-Mivtar' (*Israel Exploration Journal* 20, 1970, pp 38–59)

HARVEY, A.E., *Jesus and the Constraints of History*, The Bampton Lectures 1980 (Duckworth, London, 1982)

HAWARD, L.R.C., 'Hypnosis in the Service of Research' (Inaugural Lecture delivered at the University of Surrey, 14 February 1979)

HICK, J. (ed.), *The Myth of God Incarnate* (SCM, London, 1977)

JAUBERT, A., *The Date of the Last Supper* (trans. from French: Alba House, New York, 1965)

JEREMIAS, J., 'The Rediscovery of Bethesda', *New Testament Archaeology Monographs* I (Southern Baptist Theological Seminary, Louisville, Kentucky, 1966)

JONES, A.H.M., *The Herods of Judaea* (Oxford University Press, 1938)

JOSEPHUS, *The Jewish War* (trans. G.A. Williamson, rev. E. Mary Smallwood: Penguin, Harmondsworth, 1981)

KEE, A., *Constantine versus Christ* (SCM, London, 1982)

KENYON, F.G., 'The Text of the Bible, A New Discovery' (*The Times*, 19 November 1931, p 13)

The Chester Beatty Biblical Papyri, 8 vols (E. Walker, London, 1933-41)

KENYON, K., *Jerusalem Excavating 3,000 Years of History* (Thames & Hudson, London, 1967)

KHAN, M.F., *Deliverance from the Cross* (The London Mosque, London, 1978)

KLAUSNER, J., *Jesus of Nazareth* (Allen & Unwin, London, 1925)

KOPP, C., *The Holy Places of the Gospels* (trans. from German by Ronald Walls: Nelson, London, 1963)

KÜMMEL, W.G., *Introduction to the New Testament* (English trans. by A.J. Mattill: London, 1970)

LESSING, G.E. (ed.), *Von dem Zwecke Jesu und seiner Jünger* (G.E. Lessing, Brunswick, 1778)

MACCOBY, H., *Revolution in Judaea, Jesus and the Jewish Resistance* (Ocean Books, London, 1973)

The Sacred Executioner, Human Sacrifice and the Legacy of Guilt (Thames & Hudson, London, 1982)

MACKEY, J.P., *Jesus, the Man and the Myth* (SCM, London, 1979)

MASON, A.A., 'A Case of Congenital Ichthyosiform Erythrodermia of Brocq Treated by Hypnosis' (*British Medical Journal*, 23 August 1952, pp 422, 423)

METZGER, B., 'Recently Published Greek Papyri of the New Testament' (*Biblical Archaeologist* 10, 2 May 1947)

Manuscripts of the Greek Bible, An Introduction to Palaeography (Oxford University Press, 1981)

MØLLER-CHRISTENSEN, V., 'Skeletal Remains from Giv'at ha-Mivtar' (*Israel Exploration Journal* 26, 1976, pp 35-8)

MONTEFIORE, H., 'Jesus, the Revelation of God' (*Christ for Us Today*, pp 108-10)

MOULE, C.F.D., *The Birth of the New Testament* (A & C Black, London, 1962)

NEILL, S., *The Interpretation of the New Testament 1861-1961* (Oxford University Press, 1964)

NEIL-SMITH, C., *The Exorcist and the Possessed* (James Pike, St Ives, 1974)

NICKELL, J., *Inquest on the Shroud of Turin* (Prometheus, New York, 1983)

OESTERREICH, T.K., *Possession, Demoniacal and Other* (Kegan Paul, London, 1930)

OLMSTEAD, A.T., *Jesus in the Light of History* (Scribner, New York, 1942)

PAGELS, E., *The Gnostic Gospels* (Weidenfeld & Nicolson, London, 1980)

PINES, S., An Arabic Version of the Testimonium Flavianum and its Implications (The Israel Academy of Science and Humanities, Jerusalem, 1971)

ROBERTS, C.H., *An Unpublished Fragment of the Fourth Gospel* (Manchester University Press, 1935)

ROBINSON, J.A.T., *Honest to God* (SCM, London, 1963)
The Human Face of God (SCM, London, 1972)
Redating the New Testament (SCM, London, 1976)
Can We Trust the New Testament? (Mowbray, London, 1977)

ROBINSON, J.M. (ed.), *The Nag Hammadi Library* (Harper & Row, New York, 1977)

SARGANT, W., *Battle for the Mind* (Heinemann, London, 1957)

SCHOLEM, G., *Major Trends in Jewish Mysticism* (Schocken Books, New York, 1941)
The Messianic Idea in Judaism (Schocken Books, New York, 1971)

SCHONFIELD, H.J., *The Authentic New Testament* (Dennis Dobson, London, 1956)
The Passover Plot (Hutchinson, London, 1965)
Those Incredible Christians, A New Look at the Early Church (Hutchinson, London, 1968)

SCHREIBER, F.R., *Sybil* (Allen Lane, London, 1974)

SCHÜRER, E., *History of the Jewish People in the Age of Jesus Christ* (rev. ed. with new material by G. Vermes and F. Millar: T. & T. Clark, Edinburgh, 1973)

SCHWEITZER, A., *The Quest of the Historical Jesus, a Critical Study of its Progress from Reimarus to Wrede* (trans. W. Montgomery: A & C Black, London, 1910)

SHERWIN-WHITE, A.N., *Roman Society and Roman Law in the New Testament* (Clarendon Press, Oxford, 1963)

SIZEMORE, C. & PITTILLO, E.S., *Eve* (Victor Gollancz, London, 1978)

SMITH, J.H., *Constantine the Great* (Hamish Hamilton, London, 1971)

SMITH, M., *Clement of Alexandria and a Secret Gospel of Mark* (Harvard University Press, 1973)
The Secret Gospel (Victor Gollancz, London, 1974)
Jesus the Magician (Victor Gollancz, London, 1978)

STRAUSS, D.F., *The Life of Jesus Critically Examined* (trans. G. Eliot: Chapman, London, 1846)
New Life of Jesus (Williams & Norgate, London, 1865)

STREETER, B.H., *The Four Gospels, A Study of Origins* (Macmillan, London, 1927)

SUETONIUS, *The Twelve Caesars* (trans. R. Graves: Penguin Books, Harmondsworth, 1957)

TACITUS, *The Annals of Imperial Rome* (trans. M. Grant: Penguin Books, Harmondsworth, 1956)

THROCKMORTON, B.H. (Jr.), *Gospel Parallels, A Synopsis of the First Three Gospels* (Thomas Nelson Inc., New York, 1971)

TISCHENDORF, C. VON, *Codex Sinaiticus, Tischendorf's Story and Argument Related by Himself* (Lutterworth Press, London, 1935)

TOYNBEE, A. (ed.), *The Crucible of Christianity* (Thames & Hudson, London, 1969)

TZAFERIS, V., 'Jewish Tombs at and near Giv'at ha-Mivtar' (*Israel Exploration Journal* 20, 1970, pp 18–32)

VERMES, G., *The Dead Sea Scrolls in English* (Penguin Books, Harmondsworth, 1962)

'Quest for the Historical Jesus' (*Jewish Chronicle Literary Supplement*, 12 December 1969)

Jesus the Jew, A Historian's Reading of the Gospels (Collins, 1973, Fontana 1976: quotations from Fontana edition)

VINCENT, L.H., 'Le lithostrotos évangélique' (*Revue Biblique*, Paris, 59, 1952, pp 513–30)

WALSH, J., *The Bones of St Peter* (Victor Gollancz, London, 1983)

WARNER, M., *Alone of All her Sex, The Myth and Cult of the Virgin Mary* (Weidenfeld & Nicolson, London, 1976)

WELLS, G.A., *The Jesus of the Early Christians* (Pemberton, London, 1971)
Did Jesus Exist? (Elek/Pemberton, London, 1975)
The Historical Evidence for Jesus (Prometheus, New York, 1982)

WILSON, C., *Mysteries* (Hodder & Stoughton, London, 1978)

WILSON, I., *The Turin Shroud* (Victor Gollancz, London, 1978)

WINTER, P., *On the Trial of Jesus* (de Guyter, Berlin, 1961)

YADIN, Y., *Bar-Kokhba* (Weidenfeld & Nicolson, London, 1971)
'Epigraphy and crucifixion' (*Israel Exploration Journal*, 23, 1973, pp 18–20)
(ed.) *Jerusalem Revealed: Archaeology in the Holy City, 1968–1974* (Yale University Press & Israel Exploration Society, 1976)

ZUGIBE, F., *The Cross and the Shroud* (Angelus Books, New York, 1982)

ACKNOWLEDGMENTS

The publishers would like to thank the following for kindly supplying photographic material for reproduction:

Itzhak Amit 183 R; Bildarchiv d. Ost Nationalbibliothek 33 TL; Bodleian Library 21 TL; Werner Braun 24, 132 R; British Library 14 B, 15, 27 B; 104-5 T; British Museum 57 R, 163; Mike Busselle 42; Camera Press 183 TL; Egypt Exploration Society 21 TR; G. Ennie 175; Prof Umberto Fasola 125 T & B; Giraudon 53 T, 171 B; Sonia Halliday 85, 95 B, 111, 115 T, back cover; Robert Harding Assoc. 14 T; David Harris 47 B, 90-1; André Held 52, 146, 146-7, 161 TR; Hirmer Verlag 75 L; History Today Archives 'Alexandria: A History and a Guide' by E. M. Forster (published Whitehead Morris Ltd, Alexandria, 1938) 169 B; Michael Holford 43; Institute for Antiquity and Christianity, Claremont, California (courtesy Jean Doresse) 27 T; Israel Department of Antiquities and Museums, Jerusalem 68 T, 115 B; Israel Exploration Society (photo courtesy of Prof Nahman Avigad) 81 T; Israel Exploration Society 90, 95 T, 119 B; Karl-Geib-Museum, Bad Kreuznach 63; London Weekend Television 183 BL; Mansell/Alinari frontispiece, 47 T, 57 L, 147, 159 B, 171 T, 179 T; Mansell Collection 53 BR; Dr A.A. Mason 104 B; Ny Carlsberg Glyptothek (photo History Today) 59; Palestine Archaeological Museum 153 B: Plate No. XII, by Fred Anderegg from Erwin R. Goodenough, *Jewish Symbols in the Greco-Roman Period*, Bollingen Series 37, Vol II; *Symbolism in the Dura Synagogue* Copyright © 1964 by Princeton University Press (reprinted by permission of Princeton University Press) 73 T; Zev Radovan 75 R; Ann Ronan Picture Library 53 BL; John Rylands Library, Manchester 29 T & B; Scala 159 T, 169 T; Barrie M. Schwortz 132 L; Ronald Sheridan 45, 68 B, 68-9, 79, 101; Prof Morton Smith, Columbia University 25 T & B; Dr Patricia Smith, Hebrew University 127 T & B; Süddeutscher Verlag 33 BL & BR; University Library, Cambridge 179 B; Vatican Archives (photos courtesy of Doubleday & Co.) 156 T & B; Victoria & Albert Museum 105, 110 T & B; Weidenfeld & Nicolson Archives 81 B, 119 T, 153 T, 161 TL & B, 167; Ian Wilson 10 B; Prof Dr Hans Wulf/Evangelischer Schrifttumsdienst, Berlin 33 TR; Yale University Art Gallery/Dura Europos Collection 73 B.

Front cover: Our thanks to Father Damianos, Archbishop of St Catherine's Monastery, Sinai; to Father Gregory, Head of Sacred Council, and to the other Monks of St Catherine's Monastery for permission to publish this photograph.

INDEX

(page numbers in *italics* denote illustrations or charts)

● Marburg

● Tübingen

During the nineteenth
and early twentieth
centuries New Testament
theologians from
Tübingen, Marburg and
other German
universities challenged
traditional views on the
date and authorship of
the canonical gospels.
Some of their arguments
have required modification
in the light of recent
discoveries.

I L L Y R I C U

Arius was
banished here a
the adverse
decision at th
Council
Nica

Rome

A 'Pater Noster'
acrostic found at
Pompeii indicates
Christian presence there
prior to the town's
destruction by Vesuvius
in 79 AD.

Pompeii
Pozzuoli

'Puteoli, where we
found some brothe
(Acts 28: 14).
A Roman graffito
found here provid
one of the earliest-
known depictions
crucifixion.

M E D I T E R R A N E A

The Mark Gospel

Early tradition attests that the Mark gospel was
written in Rome, and this is accepted by most scholars.
The writer shows ignorance of Palestinian geography,
and some transparently pro-Roman sympathies.
Already by 64 AD Rome's Christians were sufficiently
numerous for Nero to blame them for the city's fire.

JESUS: THE EVIDENCE

Principal places mentioned in the text, with
locations of manuscript discoveries and likely
provenance of canonical gospels.

Scale

0	100	200 ml
0	160	320 k

The Matthew Gospel

Where the Matthew gospel was first written is
uncertain, the text exhibiting both striking semitic ar
anti-semitic features. One school of thought associate
it with Alexandria, where there were some pro-Roma
Jews, and also some very anti-Jewish Gentiles. In late
centuries Alexandrian Christians provoked
controversy for over-stressing Jesus' divinity.